Praise for Dr. Cynthia Barnett
and *I'm Not Done Yet*

"Through heart-wrenching stories, this inspiring book, chock-full of profound wisdom, vividly captures an American success story. Starting from the ground up with next to nothing on her arrival in the United States, Dr. Cynthia Barnett shares her life journey, demonstrating her strong will and determination to achieve as much as possible. And, she's not done yet!"

— Susan Friedmann, CSP,
International Bestselling Author of *Riches in Niches:
How to Make it BIG in a small Market*

"Dr. Cynthia is a woman who walks her talk. Her personal stories are inspiring and will help anyone who is serious about their dreams."

— Marcia Weider,
America's Dream Coach and
Author of *Making Your Dreams Come True*

"This is a beautifully written page-turner that had me hooked. Cynthia will inspire you to be the best you can be. Know that your best days are yet ahead!"

— Patrick Snow,
Publishing Coach and
International Best-Selling Author of *Creating Your Own Destiny*

"A powerful book by a powerful writer who knows how to reach down and touch your heart! I highly recommend it!"

— Gerry Robert,
Best-Selling Author of *The Millionaire Mindset*

"This is a wonderful book. Reading it is a transforming experience. As a teacher with an abundance of inspiration, creativity, and relevant lessons on how to live an exciting, balanced life, Dr. Cynthia is unsurpassed."

— Christian Warren,
Author of *Running with the Rhinos:
Transforming Yourself into a Leader Others Will Gladly Run With*

"Brilliant! A formidable piece of writing guaranteed to get you out of that rut and rethink your life priorities. Full of action plans to stop procrastination and set you on the track to a better life."

— Rozieta Shaary,
Best-Selling Author of *Happy Kids*

"Dr. Cynthia has inspired us with her valuable stories to share life's important lessons. This is a must read for anyone who desires to embrace life and enjoy it to the fullest."

— Linda Olson,
TEDx Speaker, #1 International Best-Selling Author
and Founder of Wealth Through Stories

"The stories in this book will inspire you to believe more deeply in your dreams and motivate you to take actions to make those dreams come true. I highly recommend it."

— Beth Dargis,
Simplicity Educator

"Dr. Barnett shares a portion of her extraordinary life in this wonderful book. From memories of her childhood on the island of St. Vincent through her "re-fired" retirement years in the United States, we get a vivid glimpse of selected experiences and life lessons she's learned growing up and growing into her later years. Her determination to shape her life to fit her dreams shows through in *I'm Not Done Yet,* propelling the reader through the book only to come to the last page wanting to apply the same principles that have undergirded the author throughout her days. Each chapter's 'I Can See Clearly Now' bonus provides an added lens of experience tempered with time, making for a double dose of a good read."

— Cindy Chatham,
Editor

"*I'm Not Done Yet* is a collection of heartfelt stories about facing your challenges and finding innovative ways to reshape events into adventures. Cynthia Barnett writes with wisdom about childhood, retirement, marriage, careers, raising children, and ultimately, staying true to one's self. Her poignant questions about life and what it can be will make readers long for their own chances to prove themselves in life's arena to see what kinds of winners they can also become."

— Tyler R. Tichelaar, PhD
Award-Winning Author of *When Teddy Came to Town*

"*I'm Not Done Yet* is an insightful and inspiring book about living life to the fullest. Dr. Cynthia inspires and delivers practical tools to help you accomplish real results."

— Toie Martin,
Author of *Living Your Life With Possibilities*

"I've had the privilege of knowing Cynthia for many years and have watched her live her dreams. She is the embodiment of the strategies she writes about. This book is the result of her working the principles she practices daily. If you want to realize your deepest desires, learn how by reading *I'm Not Done Yet.*"

— Jane Pollak,
Author of *Soul Proprietor: 101 Lessons From a Lifestyle Entrepreneur*

I'm Not Done Yet

(...And You Shouldn't Be Either)

Dr. Cynthia Barnett

AVIVA
PUBLISHING
New York

Published by:
Aviva Publishing
Lake Placid, NY, USA
(515) 523-1320
www.AvivaPubs.com

Dr. Cynthia Barnett
203-855-9714
drcynthiabarnett@gmail.com
www.RefireDontRetire.com

ISBN: 978-1-890427-79-5
Library of Congress Control Number: 2019907364

Editors: Cindy Chatman and Tyler Tichelaar
Cover Design: Meredith Lindsay
Interior Layout: Larry Alexander, Superior Book Productions
Author Photo Credit: James Ravenell

Every attempt has been made to source properly all quotes.

Printed in the United States of America

To my children and grandchildren

Acknowledgments

This book, like everything else I have created in my life, is the result of great team effort. I extend my deepest gratitude and thanks to:

My insightful editors, Tyler Tichelaar and Cindy Chatman, who provided valuable editing expertise. Your eagle eyes and attention to detail are awesome.

Susan Friedman, my publisher.

Patrick Snow, my publishing coach.

Meredith Lindsay, who designed the awesome cover.

Larry Alexander for the interior layout.

James Ravenell for taking my author photo.

Thank you for reading this book and spreading the word that our dreams are precious and essential. May your life be filled with love, joy, and abundance.

And most importantly, thank you, God, for reminding me that we are all dreamers at heart and for granting me the privilege to do this work. I am humbled and honored to serve.

Contents

Foreword

YOU HOLD WITHIN your hands a masterpiece of wisdom, wit, and insight. What a pleasure to be asked to write a foreword for such a book. You, the reader, will quickly see that the information in this book has not been developed from the "ivory tower" but in the real world. You will see very early on in this book that if you put into practice even a fraction of the strategies that are very clearly and eloquently developed, you would sing a new song in your life.

The other thing one will quickly notice by reading this great book is that the author knows what she is talking about and that the material is lived out in her life. I have such a high regard for Dr. Barnett. It's no wonder to me that she is in such demand as a speaker and as a coach to high achievers. She actually lives out the material in this book.

If you want a book that is practical, sometimes funny, sometimes touching, sometimes moving, sometimes confrontational, but always effective, to help you live a more pleasant, more effective life, then this is the book for you.

The reason I'm so proud to write the foreword for this wonderful book is that I know how many people it will help. I have read thousands of books, written several myself, and I know the power of a good book when I see one. This is one such book. Read it, highlighter in hand, and act on it.

Congratulations, Dr. Barnett, for giving the world one more reason to sing a little brighter, dance a little sweeter, and enjoy the "music" of life a little deeper.

Gerry Robert
Best-Selling Author
The Millionaire Mindset

Introduction

"You have to believe in yourself when no one else does. That's what makes you a winner."

— Venus Williams

FTER MANY RETREATS, seminars, and coaching clients, I have realized that a large percentage of people do not believe it is possible to achieve their dreams. We all possess the power to dream. Many of us have chosen not to use the power as we've gotten older, but we all had big dreams when we were little. We had visions of becoming ballerinas, singers, dancers, teachers, mothers, doctors, lawyers, and maybe even President of the United States. We played dress up and hung posters on our walls with our dream cars and mates.

What was your dream? How many times did you think to yourself, "When I grow up, I'm going to…"? Maybe you were going to buy all the candy you wanted or get a particular car. Perhaps you had a certain house in mind with a swimming pool or a boat. Maybe you wanted to help others or simply care for ten cats and dogs. But something happened along the way and you gave up on your dreams. You just quit.

A small percentage of the population did go on to achieve big dreams. What's the difference between them and you? Were their dreams more important? No. More realistic? Probably not. Were they smarter than you? Prettier? Luckier? No to all of these. But they had the burning desire to achieve their dreams; they acted in spite of their fears, and they tuned out the opinions of those who didn't encourage them.

If you've given up on your dreams, reread the previous paragraph. Which reason applies to you? Did you have a burning desire to reach your dreams? Did you let your fears prevent you from taking action? Did you believe someone who told you it wouldn't work, or look around and see other people not reaching their dreams and just assume you shouldn't reach yours? Your honest answers to these questions hold the reason why you put your dreams on a shelf. If your dreams are on a shelf, they have no chance of coming true until you pull them off and place them in the line of your focus.

What's Your Dream?

Don't fret if you can't remember what your dreams were. It's not unusual to be in the middle of adulthood and not be able to think of any dreams for yourself. Life got in the way. You got busy with the lives of others, probably because you had to. If you have trouble thinking of any dreams, you likely haven't been giving yourself enough attention. That's okay. Enjoy this book and get ready to enjoy your life more!

Right now, you probably don't have everything you need to make your dreams come true. If you did, they already would have come true. Earlier, when I mentioned the differences between those who achieve their dreams and those who don't, I never said that they knew everything they needed to know. Don't think you have to know everything, or have all the resources, or know how you're going to make your dream come true. That will come later. Bestselling author Gerry Robert said something powerful in his instructions for writing out your heart's desires: "Don't worry about whether you can afford it, if you know how to get it, or if you have other obstacles in the way. Just list what you want."

Half the fun will be the journey—watching everything come together. Remarkable things happen when you decide what you want. Opportunities will come that were probably there all along, but you don't notice them until they fit a dream you want to fulfill. When you're watching for the elements you need, life is an enjoyable experience.

I wrote this book to assist you in stretching your mind to imagine a life of new possibilities; if you put your mind to it, you can be, do, and have anything you want.

My goal is to offer practical strategies to convince you that despite the current adversities and obstacles in your life, you can indeed create and live your own dreams. Let's start this journey of self-reflection together by asking a few very important questions. Your answers to these questions will send you on a personal quest to see the truth in your life, setting you free to pursue your dreams. Taking action on the answers to these questions will give you a life of happiness, freedom, and prosperity.

- Are you frustrated that your life is not *quite* what you envisioned it to be?

- Do you wake up every morning wondering what you were born to do and why you are here on this earth?

- Are you worried about how you will spend the next twenty years?

- Are you tired of putting your dreams on the back burner, and instead, are ready to fully embrace a new adventure?

- Do you feel like a rudderless ship without direction?

- Do you have a hard time getting out of bed in the morning or falling asleep at night?

- Do you keep asking yourself, "Is this all there is?"

- Do you feel an emptiness inside that you haven't been able to fill?

- Do you wake up each morning thinking, "I want more from life.... I'm not done yet.... I have lots more to give"?

My goal is to offer practical strategies to convince you that despite the current adversities and obstacles in your life, you can indeed create and live your own dreams. Let's start this journey of self-reflection together by asking a few very important questions. Your answers will send you on a personal quest to see the truth in your life, setting you free to pursue your dreams. Taking action on the answers to these questions will give you a life of happiness, freedom, and prosperity.

That you are taking the time to read this book and apply its ideas and suggestions tells me you have what it takes to achieve your dreams. You may believe you are too young or too old, but think about it this way: You have the benefit of a fresh start with each new day. You have your whole life ahead of you to accomplish great things. Now is the time to get started moving in the right direction.

I want to help you. I will be your coach along the way, your guide, your confidant. If I can make my dreams come true, so can you. I believe in you. I believe that deep inside you, you have the power to clarify and create what you want.

What will you get from applying these practical strategies? You will learn how to harness the power of vision to transform your obstacles into opportunities. You will learn the secret to attaining lifelong happiness. You will learn to overcome rejection, expand your comfort zone, never give up, think for yourself, and follow your dreams.

I'm Not Done Yet will help you to uncover or recover your purpose so you can live a meaningful life—and there is nothing that will bring you greater fulfillment. This book will help you take real steps toward creating and achieving the dreams that matter most to you.

When you have finished reading this book and have applied the wisdom, knowledge, experience, and strategies offered here, then you will know:

- Who you really are

- How you want your life to be
- How to develop dreams that inspire you
- How to remove fear, doubt, and other obstacles

My work in my non-profit program, Amazing Girls Science, which helps young girls ignite a spark for STEAM (science, technology, engineering, art, and math), led me to receive the Inaugural AARP Purpose Prize in 2017. The national recognition from that award boosted not only my own self-confidence but broadcast to the nation the success of Amazing Girls Science. The award honors extraordinary individuals who use their life experiences to make a better future for all. What a wonderful validation of all my years of hard work! The award came with national recognition and also a financial grant, giving me the opportunity to continue the work I love: not only teaching young girls to excel academically but also inspiring retirees to fire up their own passions, revving up their motivational engines to do more during this time in their lives than they have ever done before.

The stories in this book are a compilation of some of my experiences that led me on a less-than-direct path to success. I hope they inspire you to dream bigger and reach higher. I'm sure my stories are not much different than yours. I hope that after reading mine, you will take some time to reflect on your own life and perhaps see any tough times in a new light. It really is those tough times that make us interesting and unique. Embrace those memories, draw strength from them, and learn to move on. It's not over 'til it's over! I have achieved a great deal so far, and I know my journey—and the fun—still continues.

I wonder what's around the next bend.

I'm confident that the experiences I outline in this book will prove to be valuable resources for you. These strategies have worked for me and for those who've learned them through my coaching, workshops, retreats, and keynote speeches. I know they'll work for you, provided you *take action* and apply them.

Are you ready to be the director of your life's play, the captain of your ship, and the creator of your dreams?

Are you ready to transform your own life and contribute to making the world a better place?

If so, let's enjoy this inspirational book together. Are you ready to begin? Good let's go. The realization of your dreams begins now. This is your life; this is your time, so let's get started.

Cynthia Barnett

Chapter 1

Breaking Free of Limitations

*"I will do today what others don't so I will have
tomorrow what others won't."*

— John Addison

I LOVE MY LIFE! Really! My work is rewarding to me and inspiring to others, and it really is a wonderful way to live. What more could I ask?

Don't get me wrong—arriving at this place of self-satisfaction hasn't been perfect, and it certainly hasn't been easy. I've had plenty of tough times, just like you. But I see now that those tough times led me to where I am today—fulfilled, peaceful, and grateful to know my life has meant something to others, that I have given my own unique skills and abilities to help society.

What led me here? The story goes back many years. My life, like yours, has had numerous unexpected twists and turns, and I was faced repeatedly with decisions that seemed beyond me. I often had the sensation that I was in situations way over my head. Many times I felt I had to paddle extra hard just to tread water. But once I made the decision *not* to allow myself to drown in self-pity, the next choice was to throw myself into learning how to swim so I would never again feel helpless in life's rough waters.

And learn to swim I did.

Today, my story is almost unbelievable, even to me. I, who became the assistant principal of a high school in Connecticut, was the same person who had arrived in the United States fifty years before as a young girl with no money, no friends, and no guidance. But she had one thing: a dream—a big dream. She wanted to earn the highest degree in the field of education.

This same girl had to dig in the bottom of her purse more than once for coins to take the train home to the one-bedroom apartment in the Bronx where she lived with her mother, stepfather, and two-year-old brother.

This girl cleaned houses to earn money to pay for college applications, filed documents for an insurance company to pay her share of the apartment's utilities, and waited tables in a convalescent home so she could bring home leftover food to share with her family. This girl worked in a pen factory inserting the ink into ballpoint pens, all the while dreaming that one of those same pens might help her take notes in a class and write an assignment. Maybe one day that same pen would be used to sign a job application for a local school district. All the while, this girl dreamed.

She dreamed when she was bone-tired, when her feet ached, and when her eyes crossed from too little sleep. This girl often told her family that their future would be better too—she just knew it—and then she poured a third cup of coffee to help her stay awake to study for exams the next morning. She dreamed when she wrote out checks for tuition, textbooks, and the twice-monthly grocery shopping trips. She dreamed when she received a poor grade and had to redo an assignment, when she wondered if the skipped social engagements, the missed rest, the irritable moods, and the near-empty wallet were worth the future diploma, the future classroom, and the future self-satisfaction in her own career.

She wanted a career, most certainly; she didn't want just a job. She had had enough of those; she had witnessed the dead-end, stagnant stare of friends and family who thought eight hours a day passing out tickets to the tourists back home in St. Vincent was the best life had to offer. No, this girl didn't want just a means of making money, perhaps just enough to get by. She wanted to thrive, to lose herself in a career she loved, and to eventually see the world. She wanted the double fulfillment of earning a paycheck and using her unique talents and abilities to contribute to society. She wanted to drink from the deep well of satisfaction that would come from knowing she had made a change in someone's life, that her own life and breath meant something—that would be the best possible way she could spend her days. She had only one life to live, after all, and she knew it. She wasn't willing to waste a moment.

This girl faced obstacles, of course. Everyone does. But she had lived long enough to see that not everyone faces problems in the same way. Some people look at the obstacle, determine it is too difficult to climb, and turn away. Others look at it, attempt to climb it, and then realize their own inability to conquer the mammoth problem, and also turn away. And some people study the obstacle—and study and study. They think an easy way to get to the other side must exist if they only study the obstacle long enough.

Not this girl. She saw the massive hindrance, made a few quick calculations, and ran full force and jumped. A few times, she landed back on the ground, the obstacle towering over her. Once or twice, she almost made the hurdle over, but she hit the obstacle and fell back, injured.

But she persevered. She did everything she could to encourage herself in her dream, and she allowed it to occupy her thoughts night and day, day and night. The dream of teaching young children danced before her eyes when she saw kids playing in the park, when she saw a delicate rose she could show to students, and when she read a good book with a simple but important message. She looked diligently, evaluated fairly, and became ultimately strong. She sought wise counsel, mapped out a detailed plan, and mentally practiced giving a science presentation to a classroom of attentive students. She kept the finish line in mind, always.

And one day, she jumped, and over the wall she went. Success! She was elated.

Of course, as I said, that girl was me, and I was absolutely thrilled with my accomplishment. Nothing quite matches the euphoria of achieving something that has required a great deal of work, and I unabashedly relished my achievement. But like a runner who has just completed her first 10K, I rubbed my sore calves, enjoyed a victory lap, and then set my sights on the next dream. After earning my Bachelor of Arts degree in Elementary Education and teaching fourth graders for fifteen years, I wanted to earn the highest degree possible in my field of education: a doctorate.

By that time, I was the mother of three young children, so going back to school would require a near-repeat of my earlier years of dedication and hard work. Yet I was obsessed with this new dream, and I did everything possible to keep my vision alive. I wanted most of all to contribute more to my generation—and the next—by working in the administrative field in the schools. Again, I faced obstacles and hindrances, but eventually, I walked across a platform one June afternoon and the dean of the university placed the gold tassels over my head onto my shoulders, indicating that now I could be referred to as Dr. Cynthia Barnett. I was jubilant.

For the next ten years, I worked full-time as a high school administrator and then, once again, I decided to formally close that chapter of my life. Some people referred to this time as my retirement. Funny, but I never thought of it as that. Sure, traditionally to everyone around me—family, friends, and coworkers—I was retiring. After all, I had spent a total of thirty years in education. Now was the time to relax and indulge myself in well-deserved "free" time, right?

Wrong. I still had a lot of spunk in me! So I decided I would never refer to this new chapter in my life as retirement. Instead I would refer to it as "refirement"! It worked. I still had excellent health, lots of energy, and numerous ideas on how to help and inspire others to make the most out of their lives. As I began to plan this next phase of my life, I started thinking about the events in my own journey that shaped me into who I am today.

The stories in this book are a compilation of some of my experiences that led me on a less-than-direct path to success. I hope they inspire you to dream bigger and reach higher. I'm sure my stories are not much different than yours. I hope that after reading mine, you will take some time to reflect on your own life and perhaps see any tough times in a new light. It really is those tough times that make us interesting and unique. Embrace those memories, draw strength from them, and learn to move on. It's not over 'til it's over! I have achieved a great deal so far, and I know my journey—and the fun—still continues.

I wonder what's around the next bend....

*****

I Can See Clearly Now

I can see clearly now, decades later, how these difficulties at a young age were preparing me for an adult life of teaching about empowerment, never giving up, and going after your dreams despite many obstacles and hardships, even though I was unaware of such a destiny at the time. How that destiny unfolded for me will be told in the remainder of this book.

Reflection Questions

What did you dream about doing when you were young?

_____

_____

_____

_____

Did you accomplish that dream? If so, what did you learn about yourself as a result?

_____

_____

_____

_____

If you didn't accomplish it, what can you do now to make it come true, or to pursue a new dream?

_____

_____

_____

_____

What legacy do you want to leave your family, community, or the world? How will you succeed in making that legacy a reality?

_____

_____

_____

_____

Chapter 2

Blue Uniforms

"Only those who will risk going too far can possibly find out how far one can go."

— T. S. Elliot

WHEN I WAS young and living in St. Vincent, one of the smallest islands in the Caribbean Sea, my two younger sisters, Janet and Marie, and I attended a Catholic girls' school. We were required to wear uniforms—bright blue, heavy cotton skirts and white, Peter-Pan-collared, button-down, short-sleeved blouses. White anklet socks paired with black Mary Jane shoes completed our outfits.

Every year, on the first day of school, every student arrived eager and bright, looking forward with anticipation to the new academic term. Our crisp new uniforms reflected our yearly enthusiasm, ready to accompany us during those many hours in the classroom. The uniforms had an uncanny ability to grow and change with us, being slightly scratchy and irritating at the beginning of the term and becoming softer and more comfortable as we slid into the daily, rhythmic routine of our studies.

Predictably, by the end of the school year, most of us were exhausted from the workload, tired from the lectures and homework assignments, and weary of term papers and exams. By mid-May, when our tropical spring had melted seamlessly into summer and when the deep red roses were in high bloom, most of our uniforms had faded to a dull blue, almost white, due to repeated washings and near-daily exposure to the hot island sun.

Our mother had always made our uniforms because she was a dressmaker. But when I was eleven, Mom left us in the care of her mother—my grandmother—when she headed to America in search of a better life for us. Grandma was in her fifties, which, in those days, meant she was elderly. She was glad to take care of us, of course, because she loved us, but she moved slowly and performed many of our household tasks only minimally. So as the eldest child, I helped in many of the caretaking responsibilities of the younger ones.

We weren't poor by any means, but we certainly weren't rich, and we knew Mom was doing her best across the ocean to eventually provide something better for us.

As we neared the end of one school year, when I was about twelve years old, I realized that not only was Mom not able to make us new uniforms for the following school year, but that Grandma was hinting to me that no money was available even to purchase the fabric. I glanced down at my faded skirt and my limp white blouse and intuitively knew that, come August, if I had to wear the same uniform, everyone at school would know we were poor.

Even if our uniforms fit somewhat, which was possible but unlikely, the faded blue color would shout loud and clear that the skirts belonged to last year, and I just knew my sisters and I would be talked about behind our backs, pitied with whispers and sideways glances. I would not only be known as "the poor girl whose mother left," but perhaps also excluded from all future social invitations because my circle of friends might think I was unable to provide any extra gifts, so they wouldn't want to embarrass me. My mind reeled with the ramifications of showing up on the first day of school in that dull blue cotton skirt.

I didn't know what to do because our only income was Grandma's small allowance from my uncle, which we used for food and necessary household expenses, and the occasional few dollars Mom sent from America to help. I reasoned that we could save those few dollars she sent to purchase those new uniforms. Or, at least, we would buy the fabric and take it to the dressmaker in town.

We received mail from America only once a week, on Wednesdays, so every Tuesday night, I would go to sleep thinking, "Tomorrow. Tomorrow we will open the mail and find money for new fabric." The worry would subside, and I would rest peacefully. But then, on Wednesday night, when all the envelopes had been opened, the letters read, and the bills stacked high, the disappointment of not even a few enclosed dollars would spiral me back down into discouragement, and I would bite my lip to hold back my tears in front of Janet, Marie, and Grandma. By Friday, hope began to stir again, and by the following Tuesday, I would be full of expectation, laughing with my sisters and reassuring Grandma that everything would be all right.

On Wednesday afternoon, with anticipation rising, I would run to the mailbox with my fingers crossed, put the key in the lock, and pull down the mailbox tab. Gathering the stack of envelopes in my hands, I would quickly shuffle through them, looking for that one blue envelope with the stamp from America pasted in the upper right-hand corner. But no blue envelope appeared, so I went through the stack again, willing myself to slow down. Surely, Mom had written to us.

I knew that hearing from Mom meant more than receiving money for new clothes. She was away from us just as we were away from her, and the pain was mutual. Our hearts longed to be together, and we all knew she was sacrificing her presence with us so she could one day, somehow, provide something better and more secure for her family. But as a young girl, I could see Mom only in my mind's eye, leaning over bright blue fabric, snipping and cutting the cloth and threading her needle while she sat in the living room's corner window seat every August, making those new skirts.

The end of the term was quickly coming to a close. We had not heard from Mom in two weeks, then three. We only had eight weeks between terms, and my hopes for new uniforms were slowly dying, just like my pens had run out of ink and my erasers had dissolved on my math papers.

Still, in those quiet moments before sleep came every night, all I could think of was how, on the first day of school, my classmates with brand new uniforms would take one look at me and my sisters and laugh. "What happened, girls? Did you forget that school was starting? Or did you just lose your new skirts already?" The sneer in their voices would be unmistakable; I could just imagine their derision.

Now it was Week Four; we had not heard from Mom in four weeks. The hot July sun reminded me that, with only four weeks left before the first day of school, the dressmaker in town was already stitching furiously, booked for weeks in advance to make the new uniforms for my classmates. Even if by some miracle we had the money and could purchase the fabric, we knew of no one else we could hire to sew the skirts.

Now Wednesday had come around once more, and although these afternoons were usually marked with disappointment, I took the mailbox key from its hook in the kitchen and went to the mailbox, recognizing that a glimmer of hope still flickered in me about receiving some money. Perhaps today I would see that blue envelope with the USA stamp in the corner. I put the key into the lock and pulled down the tab. *Mail!* Envelopes were piled high in the gray box! I shoved the key into my pocket and reached for the papers. Was that a blue envelope I saw? It was! Relieved, I realized I had been holding my breath. Smiling broadly, I closed the mailbox and, still holding the key in my hand, ran through the back door into the house. I would share the good news with everyone at the same time.

"Mail from America!" I shouted as I burst into the living room. Throwing the other envelopes onto the hall table, I plopped down on the sofa while Janet and Marie ran to sit beside me. Grandma's face softened as she lowered herself into the chair by the window, looking almost like a little child on Christmas morning. Oh, what would Mom say? *And,* not at all feeling guilty, I asked myself, *how much money did she send?*

Excitedly, I ripped open the envelope, looking for the familiar crisp American dollar bills. At first I saw nothing at all in the envelope, certainly not the deep green of the money I was expecting. Then I saw the folded paper. A letter.

I glanced quickly through the correspondence, my mother's familiar handwriting bringing her voice into the air. I took a deep breath and read her words aloud.

Dear Ones,

I miss you so much! I know that you opened this letter, expecting to find money, and it breaks my heart to tell you I have none to send you. My landlord has raised my rent, and though I have been looking for a second job every evening, I have yet to find one. I had only a few dollars left for food after I paid the bills. I'm so, so sorry.

I promise to send money as soon as I can. Kiss each other for me and know that I love and miss you all.

Love,
Mom

I could no longer hold it in. With tears streaming down my face, I ran into my bedroom, closed the door, covered myself up with the pink and white quilt on my bed, and cried and cried. Despair, dejection, sadness, and disappointment all blended together into sobs, heaves, and a broken heart.

The days wore on. School would be starting in just two days. I no longer looked forward to Wednesdays, and I let Janet check the mailbox now. I had held countless conversations with myself about the uniform situation, telling myself sternly that I was really too old to be concerned about this; Mom was working hard, and that was all that mattered. The skirts still fit us, surprisingly, and the white blouses could be bleached and starched to look almost acceptable. Even the white anklets were darned and ready for wear.

Yet, for all my efforts to push away the expected humiliation on that first day of school, I still felt tortured, imagining all the other children laughing and making fun of us in our faded uniforms. That night as I prepared for bed, I realized I had never actually heard any student being teased about a faded skirt, but I also knew my classmates could be cruel; I had heard them talk privately about other students, and I just knew Janet and Marie and I would be their next targets. I had better simply talk with my sisters in the morning; perhaps I could explain what might happen when they didn't fit in with their friends, when the entire school would think we were poor, and what we could do when the other students laughed at us. I climbed under the pink and white quilt, quietly weeping, and forced myself to smile. Sadness had become my near-constant companion, and I knew that tomorrow I must not let my sisters know just how sad I was. Best to practice that smile now so it would look natural.

I turned out the light and determinedly closed my eyes, willing myself to sleep. Then, without warning and absolutely out of thin air, an idea popped into my head. *Why don't you go back and look at those uniforms?* Wait! What? Where did that thought come from? But it was a new thought, and I didn't question it. I dried my tears on the quilt, rolled out of bed, and went to my closet. I opened the door and took out my uniform, then unclipped the faded blue skirt from the hanger and held it in my hands. Slowly, I ran my fingers over the waistband. Then I unbuttoned it and brought down the zipper. With my head still not comprehending anything specific, I turned the skirt inside out. *Brilliant blue stared back at me!* I looked again, unbelieving, and turned the skirt once more back and forth, inside out and outside in. The truth finally emerged into my swirling thoughts: the inside of the fabric was *unfaded*—it was bright and looked brand new!

A plan began to form in my mind. Mother had left her sewing basket at home when she had gone to America. I went to the closet once again and pulled the basket off the shelf. Going back to my bed, I opened the basket and pulled out the old shears. Taking a deep breath, I turned the skirt inside out, smoothed it carefully on my bed, and aimed the points of the shears at the small stitches. *Careful now,* I told myself. *I mustn't clip the fabric.* Slowly, painstakingly, I snipped away at the blue thread, one stitch at a time, until the three pieces of the skirt lay apart on the pink and white quilt. I stepped back and gazed at them. The waistband, zipper, and skirt gazed back.

Silent, I waited. I had little experience with sewing—Mom had always done that—but she taught me when I was younger how to thread a needle and perform a basic stitch on small pieces of fabric to make clothes for my doll, and I remembered that she had also taught me how to sew on a button.

I knew what I had to do.

Using my sister's uniform skirt as the pattern, I began to work. I picked up the pieces of cut-apart fabric, walked to the living room, and cleared the surface of the cabinet that housed the old treadle sewing machine. I sat down on the small chair that rested beside it. Could I remember how Mom threaded the machine? Laying the pieces of fabric aside, I fingered the large black metal instrument, moving the parts gingerly and opening the small drawers in the cabinet that held small sewing supplies and, yes! A bobbin! Slowly, deliberately, I wound the bobbin from the spool of thread on the spool holder and then I guided the black thread through the hooks and tension regulator and, ultimately, through the machine needle. Now to bring up the bobbin thread. Amazed at myself and feeling somewhat guided by Mom's presence, I turned the hand wheel with my right hand while holding the upper thread in my left. I was stunned to see the bobbin thread pull up just as I had remembered. I pulled both threads to the back, picked up two pieces of fabric, and matched the right sides together. I turned the hand wheel to lower the needle into the fabric, reached behind to lower the presser foot, and slowly moved my feet on the treadle, faintly remembering the rhythm I saw when Mom pushed forward first one foot, then the other. The fabric moved forward; I was sewing! Brief images of Mother at the machine now came rushing back to me; step by step, at midnight now, I reversed the pleats, hemmed the skirt, and reattached the waistband—the trickiest part of the entire job.

After several hours, I was staring at a bright blue skirt, looking for all the world as if it were brand new.

I was absolutely ecstatic about my success. With renewed determination, I drank in the confidence that I could tackle the other two skirts, and for the rest of the night and all the next day, I snipped threads, turned fabric, pinned piece to piece, and pedaled, watching the marvel of the needle going up and down, stitching my dashed hopes and dreams back together. The following evening, Grandma handed me the washed and pressed uniforms, and I hung them on hangers on our closet doors, ready to be donned in the morning. They looked brand new.

Something happened to me with that experience. I had never felt as low as I did when I thought we were destined to look poor. And now here I was, feeling such pride about figuring out how to do something with what little we had. I felt oddly grown-up, knowing I had faced what seemed an insurmountable problem, had come up with a solution, and had implemented it just before a deadline! The sense of accomplishment was exhilarating. When school started the next day, Janet, Marie, and I stepped proudly into our classrooms wearing bright blue, crisp uniforms. I felt like I was walking on air, so proud of myself. Only my sisters and grandmother knew the story behind those bright blue skirts. I felt empowered somehow, like I had pulled off something nobody knew about—and nobody needed to know. We had solved the problem ourselves. Mom was working hard and so were we. We would be all right. Wearing that bright blue skirt, feeling it brush against my knees when I sat down in my chair in the classroom that September morning, I knew my uniform not only represented a new year to me; today it represented new strength, an invincibility that was new to my character, something no one could take away from me.

Eagerly, I pulled out my books, ready to begin another term.

*****

I Can See Clearly Now

Looking back, I see that this event marked the awakening of an inner resilience to life's difficulties. I began to develop problem-solving skills, and my attitude shifted from accepting hard circumstances as inevitable to looking at them as if they were puzzles to be solved with creativity. I also made an inner commitment never to give up on a challenge. These abilities and decisions would prove to be absolutely essential to facing other obstacles in my life. I knew I would always remember the story of the Blue Uniforms, and I would hope.

Reflection Questions

When have you proven yourself resilient in the face of adversity?

_____

_____

_____

_____

How did that experience help you when you faced future obstacles?

_____

_____

_____

_____

What problem might you be facing now that you can draw upon that resiliency to solve?

_____

_____

_____

_____

Chapter 3

Land of the Brave

*"There are two ways to live your life. One is
as though nothing is a miracle. The other is as
though everything is a miracle."*

— Dr. Albert Einstein

I CLOSED AND LOCKED the front door behind me,
listening carefully for the double-click that assured me
the key had turned the inside lever. My throat tightened
unexpectedly: This might be the last time I would see the
dwelling where I had spent my entire childhood.

I had already walked through the small, two-bedroom
house, making sure I had picked up every last item I would
need for my journey. As I walked through the bedroom
I had shared with my two younger sisters, I knew I was
saying goodbye to the room itself—to the high window that
framed two palm trees that towered above the house next
door, to the double bed that now would engulf my little

sister alone—no more unconscious kicks from her at night, and no more complaints that she had lost sleep because of my occasional snoring. I glanced at the small rug, hand-woven by local artisans and purchased on a whim with my waitressing money. I loved the bright red and orange colors swirled with specks of yellow. Everything in the room spoke of my growing-up years. I bowed my head and closed the door, silently paying homage to the walls that had heard my childish giggles and my adolescent whispered prayers, the same walls that had beheld my aching heart full of homesickness for my mother and housed my moody tears as I grew into young womanhood. I glanced at Grandma's room, the door open as always. I moved from the hallway and walked to the kitchen to get a last drink of water. Slowly, I let my gaze take it all in. The picture on the refrigerator—a doodle I had scribbled while chatting with a girlfriend when I was eleven and that Grandma had thought "really quite remarkable"—seemed to grin back at me as I smiled at the memory of that conversation. My friend and I had been talking, of course, about boys, and my latest crush had just looked at me that afternoon and waved, and I had been thrilled. My eyes rested on the kitchen table—how many nights had I sat at the little dinette to work on an assignment? How many mornings did I brush toast crumbs off my papers as I finished a rushed breakfast before class? And how many lovely, ordinary dinners had I shared around that table with my beloved grandmother and my two sisters and brother?

Could I really leave? Was I really saying goodbye to all this? I turned and moved through the living room, heading for the front door. I had been preparing for weeks for this departure, but I couldn't hurry my steps even if I had wanted to. The living room had its own memories. Here is where I had visited with my cousins, laughed with my aunts and uncles, and practiced the piano. Here is where I had put up my feet when I chatted with Grandma during our late-night talks and where my sisters and I had sprawled on the floor to play jacks and put together puzzles.

My suitcase was already in the car. I mentally went through my checklist: baggage tagged with my new address, jacket for the air-conditioned plane—*How odd it will be*, I thought, *to be cool after the perpetual warmth of St. Vincent.* My purse—now I thought carefully—passport, yes, thirty dollars cash, yes. The small card with Mom's address written in black ink, carefully printed by my own hand, lay in the zippered pocket inside my small, navy blue shoulder bag along with my identification. And my flight itinerary, folded in half and in half again, nearly torn as I had folded and unfolded it so many times, crinkled in my firm grasp. I had dreamt about the meaning—the reality—of that itinerary. The paper verified I was really, truly leaving the island, the first tangible object indicating the first steps of a dream.

The summer sun sang its beautifully quiet, lazy ballad that early afternoon in July 1963. Immediately I could feel its warmth reflected on the soles of my feet, through my leather sandals. I had always loved that sensation. Whenever I had ventured off the island—which was rare—that warmth through my shoes had always signaled "home" to me. "Three steps down and four to the car!" How many times had I singsonged that phrase as a child? I remembered jumping down the stairs with both feet and then hopping like a rabbit to the car, all the while saying the words to the rhythm of my own personal drumbeat.

Grandma was already in the front passenger seat, my two younger sisters and brother in the back, and Uncle Thomas, who would slip into the driver's seat in a moment, gallantly held the back door for me. I curtsied dramatically. "Well, thank you, kind sir!" I said with a British accent. Then I tossed my overnight bag at my sister and told her, keeping the quiver out of my voice, "Scoot over, Squirrel!" She stuck out her tongue at me and scooted.

The airport was an hour away, and all our words having been said, the car ride was quiet. I watched Sam, the neighbor boy, hold his ball after it dropped from the hoop nailed onto the garage frame. He recognized our car and waved to me as we drove by. When we crossed Alexander Street, I saw Mrs. Murphy, my eighth grade science teacher, out on her own front porch watering her cherished roses. She had always had a vase of those Mr. Lincoln reds on her desk in the classroom every single day.

I settled back in my seat. Enough reminiscing. *Look forward, Cynthia.*

The plane was scheduled to leave at 5 p.m., and I knew that, because of my unfamiliarity with the airport—I had never flown before—I would feel more at ease about the flight if I wasn't rushed. My family had agreed and now, after their final goodbyes, I would be boarding Flight #241, departing St. Vincent Island Municipal Airport.

In a little over an hour, we arrived, and in one glance, I took in the activity of our small but lively airport. Planes of all sizes and kinds moved slowly in and out of their assigned parking spaces, as if they were simply cars at a shopping mall. Uncle Thomas maneuvered the Buick into an available space, shifted the car into park, and turned off the engine. We all sat a moment, silent. Then I took a deep breath and opened my door. I lifted my suitcase out of the trunk and settled the strap of my overnight bag onto my shoulder. Then I and my small entourage made our way to the desk inside the terminal. I had been to the airport a few times to pick up Mom when she arrived, but I had never been in the position to be the one departing.

I knew what to do—I had talked with my cousin Cecily extensively about every detail of the flight—so I walked confidently up to the information desk and presented my identification and passport to the airport clerk. She pleasantly chatted with me while she tagged my suitcase, lifted it to a wheeled cart and, with a wave of her hand, motioned me toward my boarding gate. The entourage moved when I did.

I smiled. I was traveling to America, and I knew I took with me a little bit of the heart of every person who had come to see me off. My mother had been in the United States for seven years, working and sending money home so that eventually we could all be united in her adopted country. And now I was going to join her in "the land of the free."

How I loved that term! We were free in St. Vincent, of course, but our freedom was somewhat limited. I had learned that, in America, people were free to explore, to work, and to follow their own dreams. Poverty wasn't around every corner like it was on the back streets of the island, and opportunity for adventure—both professional and personal—was gloriously abundant, or so I had heard. Most of what I knew for certain came from my mother, who was working as a dressmaker—she even made beautiful dresses for us and sent them through the mail—and who, by her hard work and in her frequent letters, kept the hope alive that we would one day join her. Now, as the oldest child—I was all of nineteen years old—I was the first to cross the Atlantic Ocean in a Boeing 747 jumbo jet to go live with her.

I tucked my passport back into my purse and looked around. Several friends had followed our car and now joined us in the terminal. As I smiled and hugged each one in turn, I was surprised to feel my eyes watering. *Oh, no!* I had determined—absolutely forbidden myself—that I not cry when I said my goodbyes. I knew that in some way, to every single person who smiled at me—some through trembling lips—I represented them. Each sibling, cousin, neighbor, and friend had a part inside them that also wondered what life was like off the island or, better said, beyond the island. St. Vincent was small, intimate. And we all loved it for that. But we also knew the familiar, the safe, and the predictable. Life on the island, for the most part, remained the same for generations. Industry came and went, children grew up to graduate, marry, and have children who, like their mothers and fathers, would enjoy the light amber sand that slipped under the emerald green water lapping the shore. The locals would sit around tables on the patios of local restaurants after closing hours just to watch the moon rise, listening to the quiet lullaby of the evening waves.

I knew I was leaving home. But I was also leaving home to *go* home. Mom was waiting for me, and I had missed her profoundly. I had been only twelve when she had climbed up the steps to a jumbo jet, and in her absence, I had grown into a young woman. Seeing her twice during that time was painfully sweet, like hopping from one stepping stone to another over a brook to get to the other side. No time to stand on one of those stones to admire the beauty of the moving water or listen to its song. Written correspondence had to bridge the days between the stepping stones. But I knew Mom trusted me and was proud of my achievements at school. She knew I would not be a burden, and I wanted nothing more than for her to be pleased with the adult I had become. When I arrived at the small apartment she rented on the outskirts of the city, I knew I would settle in quickly and get a job, contributing to the apartment expenses as an adult was expected to do.

But Mom herself had tasted the exotic spice of American freedom, and she knew I had my sights set on adventures of my own. She was only too pleased to encourage me to explore my new world for any direction I might want to go.

I reserved my last hug for Grandma. She had given up so much for me; she had given so much *to* me, and now, in some way, I could sense she was giving me away. Like a bird she had nurtured for seven years, she now lifted her wings so that I could fly on my own—fly across the ocean to meet the link between us: her daughter, my mother.

I blew kisses to everyone and turned away, my eyes blurring once again. Intentionally, I lifted my head so my loved ones would not think I was too insecure to make the trip. Indeed, as I started the walk toward the huge plane—about a seventy-five-yard trek—I felt I was embarking on a ten-mile hike. Time slowed, like in the movies, and I had to mentally tell myself to put one foot in front of the other. Now here was the portable stairway, with fourteen steps, in front of me. I grasped the handrail and climbed up and up and up. At the top of the landing, I turned back to look at my family and friends who, I knew, were still watching from the "Waving Gallery," the area reserved for people to see off their loved ones. It was the unspoken custom of the day to take someone to the airport and wait hospitably for the plane to taxi. When the aircraft began its ascent into the sky, the family would wave wildly, believing that through the tiny airplane window their loved one could see the final farewell. I knew this would be the last moment they could see me clearly. From the top step of the stairway, I turned and waved one last goodbye, and then I ducked my head to enter the plane.

The small propeller plane would take me to Trinidad where I would change planes for the second leg of my journey. I quickly found a seat, settled in, and waited for further instructions. Never having flown before, I was both fascinated and apprehensive about being in an aircraft not tethered to land. I found the noise of the engine much louder than I had anticipated, and the ride, to perfectly match the description my friends had given me of air travel, was "bumpy"—quite the appropriate word for turbulence. I worked to make sense of knowing something flying in the air could encounter "bumps." I grinned to myself at the thought.

Once we landed, I quickly gathered my belongings and followed the crowd since everyone seemed to know where they were going. As we approached the gate, I pulled out my well-folded itinerary to make sure I was in the correct place, and soon I was climbing another set of steps to another plane, the jumbo jet that would take me to America. I looked down to watch my step between the stairs and the plane and then looked up.

Oh, my! My hand involuntarily flew to my mouth. I was in the biggest bus *ever*! I smiled. My surprise at the enormity of the cabin had unexpectedly calmed some of my pre-flight jitters. At least that's what I called them. But once I had found my seat, pushed my bag under the seat ahead of me, and leaned back to get my bearings, the jitters increased. The flight attendant shut the door, and the plane began to taxi down the runway.

Now the more accurate word came to mind: fear. I was downright scared. Not of flying—I found the idea of moving through the air at an unbelievably fast speed tremendously exhilarating—but the closing of the airplane door clanged with a sort of finality, like the period at the end of a sentence. My life on St. Vincent had come to an end, period.

Suddenly, my head swam. *What in the world was I doing? I knew almost everyone in St. Vincent and nearly everyone knew me. And they loved me! I was just plain crazy to get in this huge thing—how in the world could such a heavy piece of machinery stay in the air, after all?—and go to a place I've only heard of! Nice acting, Cynthia! You have absolutely no idea what you're doing!*

My fear had been growing for several weeks, though I had done my best to hide it. After all, I *was* nineteen and a grown woman. But the unknownness of the upcoming change in my life had silently grown alongside my excitement as I made arrangements to leave. I had refused to call it "fear," but I had also caught myself numerous times purposefully slowing my breath when my heart beat faster at the thought of leaving everything familiar—people and places—for the completely unfamiliar world of New York. Oh, yes, I had heard of America, but hearing is not the same as knowing. Mental images flitted through my imagination: I saw myself losing the card with Mom's address on it, and panic rose up in me. I had taken care of that disturbing image by memorizing her address. Then I thought of waiting in the huge airport in New York if Mom was delayed in picking me up. *What would I do?* I rehearsed a tentative plan in my mind, but the questions kept pushing away any effort to think clearly. Because I had lived on the island all my life, was I backward and ignorant about city life? Would passersby smile pityingly at me when they detected the remnants of my Caribbean accent? Were my clothes fashionable enough that I wouldn't stand out in a crowd as a newcomer? I had heard that thieves often scouted for people who looked like tourists, unsure of their destination. I struggled to keep my apprehensions private, and I asked myself for the umpteenth time if I was ready for this unknown chapter in my life. Yes, I was most definitely uneasy about starting a new life in America, yet I took distinct comfort in knowing I was journeying to "the land of the brave." I would be in America; I would be brave. I *would be* brave, and I would start practicing that bravery now.

The six-hour plane ride ahead of me seemed tremendously long, but already passengers were turning their heads and shoulders, maneuvering into comfortable positions in which to sleep. Apparently, plane rides can be quite uneventful. The ordinariness of it all calmed me somewhat. I set my mind on my immediate surroundings to drive away further anxiety. *Think, Cynthia!*

First of all, I was astonished to realize I really was in a huge aircraft in the sky, high above the clouds. I listened intently to every word the flight attendant said, quickly memorizing the demonstrated instructions about emergency landings. *Really? My seat turns into a flotation device?* I pushed away the unwelcome image of me floating in the sea, desperately holding on to the deep burgundy cushion. I diverted my attention to the young mother with the three-year-old holding a doll. There, that was better. I took a deep breath. I was getting pretty good at averting those disturbing thoughts. Soon, the flight attendant served a meal. I was fascinated at the orderly presentation of dinner to people seated in such close quarters. The food was, as Grandma used to say, "nothing to write home about," but I was grateful to have something to eat. In my excitement and pre-flight nervousness, I had skipped breakfast and lunch so my stomach was growling.

After three hours of staring out over the wing of the plane into the vast sky of clouds and ocean, I found myself nodding off, and I smiled as I drifted into a light sleep, thinking I was finally getting the hang of being an airline passenger. I was pleasantly surprised when, before I knew it, the flight attendant was coming down the aisle, quietly waking the passengers, reminding them to bring their seats upright. We would be landing soon.

Really? We were almost in America? I could feel my heartbeat speed up again. Quickly, I adjusted my seat, rolled my neck to get out its crick and rubbed my eyes, really only to make sure I wasn't dreaming. I was almost to the United States! I would see Mom in just a little while.

I looked out the window once again, this time to see, far below, the city lights flickering in the night sky. The plane banked and the voice on the intercom informed us that we were approaching Kennedy International Airport. "Please make sure your seatbelt is buckled and your trays are in the upright position. We will be landing in just a few minutes. Welcome to America." The flight attendant was sweetly sincere, knowing that, for a few of us, this was our maiden voyage to the home of the red, white, and blue.

The plane banked again, and suddenly coming into view were the beautiful lights of New York City, outlining the skyscrapers and coastline. *The lights!* There must have been millions and millions of lights!

The plane was making its descent. The buildings grew bigger, the neon signs and the blinking marquee illuminated the city streets. *Bump!* Startled, I grabbed the armrest. Then I realized the plane had just landed, and I relaxed my grip. The buildings now flashed past my window as the pilot braked the plane, and only one thought pushed itself to the surface of my mind: *I was in America.*

Breathless with anticipation, I started looking for my mother through the plane window. I naively thought I might get a glimpse of her in some building before we disembarked. The plane turned again, this time away from the terminal, and taxied on the runway for another ten minutes before coming to a complete stop. I exhaled, realizing I had been holding my breath. Even though I was excited, I found profound relief washing over me when all motion halted: We were on solid ground once again.

The seatbelt light in the ceiling flashed and softly hit its high ping. As if on cue, the sound of many seatbelts being unfastened at once filled the air, and the passengers rose from their seats almost simultaneously, opening the overhead compartments to reach for carry-on luggage. I remained seated, however, and wondered silently if the word "traffic" applied to people too.

When I could move freely, I stood, picked up my bag, and walked to the plane's open door. This time as I stood on the top step of the moveable platform, I paused for a moment to take in the view. All I could see was a sea of white faces—I had never seen so many white people in my life! The people of St. Vincent are 98 percent of African descent, our skin color dark brown, so I simply was unused to such a visual panorama of another race. I glanced around the airport—so much hustle and bustle with people coming and going! I glanced to my right and was momentarily awed by the number of cars, bumper to bumper, on the freeway. I knew without a doubt that my world was about to change dramatically.

But first, I must find the familiar smile. I stood on tiptoe, scanning the crowd. There! I quickened my pace.

I couldn't wait to be in her arms again.

*****

I Can See Clearly Now

"Welcome to life in the United States!" My mother's whispered words would forever be connected in my heart to a myriad of emotions. The awe, excitement, intimidation, and self-doubt of starting a new life in a new land all blended together with a peaceful sense of once again being with family. I was not alone, and I was blissfully in the presence of one who loved me and encouraged me in this foreign endeavor.

I knew America promised me great opportunity if I only had the fortitude to give back to it hard work. I knew I had a determined willingness to learn the culture of my new homeland, and that my innate stubbornness would serve me well. After all, I was the newcomer here, and I did not expect America—or Americans—to simply give me all the wonderful opportunities I had heard about. The land itself—its history and melting pot of people, its laws and its privileges—had welcomed me warmly, and now it was up to me to express my thanks appropriately. I was here, and I was humbled not only by my mother's years of labor to bring me to the country, but also by the American idea of trust. America trusted her people to accept the challenge of dreaming dreams, of working hard to make those dreams come true, of working side by side with people from around the world. The United States was built on the idea of respect—its constitution stated that its citizens respected God-given rights—and so the people respected each other in speech, in religion, in taking care of their families, as equals. Or such was the ideal. I was not naïve; I knew I would most likely face some challenges in being a newcomer. But mostly, I planned to give back to America the same respect it was giving me—the opportunity to learn and grow, to honor others and help them move forward in their dreams, too. Over the next several decades, I would come to characterize my abundant life in this new country by three most-descriptive words—one I created myself—that summarize the personal gifts America gave to this nineteen-year-old, now-turned grandmother. These words capture the spirit of the USA to me: reinvention, refirement, and renewal.

Not a bad description of a wonderful life in a wonderful land.

Reflection Questions

What leaps of faith have you taken such as leaving home or a comfortable situation to pursue your dream?

_____

_____

_____

_____

What gratitude do you feel for that experience, regardless of how it turned out?

_____

_____

_____

_____

What opportunities are you grateful for that your country provides for you?

_____

_____

_____

_____

What three words would you use to describe the positive aspects of your spirit?

_____

_____

_____

_____

Chapter 4

Rejection Roundabout

"It is not the mountain we conquer, but ourselves."

— Sir Edmund Hillary

GROWING UP IN St. Vincent, I always felt somewhat isolated. Mom would write us letters from America, and I knew from my studies at school that the world held dreams and opportunities not available to me on the island. Grandma was getting older, Mom seemed to be settled in her new job in the States, and my sisters and brother had already mentioned their eagerness to travel the world and experience new cultures. St. Vincent was home, yet something pulled at me, a desire to push myself beyond what I could see, to make my life count for something more than just graduating only to work at a day job while Janet and Marie finished school.

During my high school years, fueled by American influence in our news and among my relatives, I began to think the best way I could make a difference in the world was to pursue higher education. I talked with several of my instructors at the Catholic girls' school I attended, and they unanimously urged me to continue with my studies, agreeing that I would have the best opportunity if I attended a college in the United States.

And so I arrived at my decision to go to an American university. My dream was simply to get the best education possible. But I didn't have any money, and I didn't have the slightest idea how to begin the search for a particular college. Nor did I know anything about the process of being accepted into a college. But I had my own unique way of getting information: I began asking questions of everyone I met.

Aunt Mary, what is college like?

Mr. Brown, you graduated from college; how did you get in?

Hello, Robert! Would you tell me again the title of the person who accepts applications?

Mrs. Abernathy, what must I do now to prepare for the application process?

I was in my senior year of high school then, and I knew the term would be over in the blink of an eye, so I needed a plan or I would be like many of the islanders, earning a minimum wage at drink stands, serving the tourists. Although steady work was to be admired, I had my sights set higher, so I knew I must get a move-on if I were to go further in life and not be dissuaded from going to America.

Although Grandma would be sorry to see me go, I knew Janet, Marie, and Roy were helping more around the house now and that Grandma, in her declining health, would have adequate care. Plus, I wanted desperately to be a role model for my sisters and brother, showing them that they, too, could break out of the island mentality, one that spoke of working just to get by, to marry and have children, and to repeat the cycle. Naturally, nothing was expressly wrong with that; I just didn't want to become trapped into thinking my mind would regress after I graduated because I had stopped learning. To me, to stop learning would be the greatest of all tragedies.

I graduated in mid-June. A week later, after I explained in the last chapter, having saved my money and received the blessing of my grandmother, sisters, and brother, I left to join my mother in the United States of America. I was so excited! Once I was settled with a current address, I could begin the college application process. Although I could have remained in St. Vincent and applied for colleges by mail, I wanted to secure employment, establish residency, and be available for personal interviews when the time came.

Eventually, after asking more questions, I understood the application process clearly. Next step: Send away for applications. That was easy. Then, when they came in the mail, I was taken aback. *Filling out these forms was a test in itself!* I was momentarily bewildered. Question after question and line by line, I completed each application meticulously, answering the essay questions only after writing out several drafts on scratch paper. Grandma had taught us that first impressions were difficult to change. I wanted each application—my first impression—to speak of my sincere desire to answer each question fully, yet concisely, with few if any corrections.

I was living with my mother and working part-time at a local restaurant in New York. I spent most evenings researching colleges and completing applications. The application fees alone indicated my own personal sacrifice. With every check I wrote, I remembered the hours I spent waiting tables. All in all, I applied to seven different colleges, mailing all the applications in mid-October, hoping to work for a year and officially enroll the following fall.

And then I waited.

By February I had received my first rejection letter. *Okay, that's to be expected.* I steadied myself while I held the official college stationery. I couldn't be a student at every school anyway; I needed only one college to accept me, and I really didn't have my heart set on any particular one. Two weeks later, I received the second letter declining my admission. Then the third one arrived, and then the fourth. My hopes began dropping. Had I misunderstood something about the process? How could I be rejected again? One week later, I received rejection letters from the fifth and sixth colleges. And then, one rainy afternoon in March, I opened the envelope from the last college and saw the familiar wording, "We thank you for your application and regret to inform you that you have not been selected to enroll...." I went to my room, shut the door, lay down on my bed, and cried. All seven colleges had rejected my applications. Not only had I sacrificed my hard-earned money for nothing, but my self-esteem was battered beyond anything I could remember. Perhaps I was not college material after all. Perhaps this was a sign that I would never be able to complete college-level classes, that maybe my island education had not adequately prepared me for American universities, that the content would be too difficult for me. I wondered if I simply wasn't smart enough to excel at university work. Perhaps I should just return to St. Vincent and give up my dream of being a college graduate.

Not long after I received the last notification letter, I spoke casually with an acquaintance about my circumstances. She heard the despair and discouragement in my voice.

"Cynthia, didn't you tell me that you play the piano?" she asked, reminding me of a past conversation.

"Yes, I do play; I began taking piano lessons when I was seven years old," I answered, not understanding why she had asked.

"Perhaps you could apply to a music school." She looked at me intently. "With that many years of music education in your experience, you might be accepted there. It won't be the same as a university education, but it would be higher education nonetheless, and you might find it a worthwhile avenue to pursue."

I remember politely thanking her, but I had absolutely no desire to pursue a music career. My heart lay in teaching, and I really wanted eventually to instruct young children all about the world. Plus, I enjoyed playing the piano, but

I didn't really *love* it. Surely, to be accepted into a music school, you must *love* music.

But the suggestion would not go away. The thought of music school began to mingle with the disappointment of the seven college rejection letters at home. Soon new ideas began to stir in my head. *Could* I learn to love music? Would I have the stamina to take up practicing again, up to three or four hours a day? Would getting a degree in music satisfy my deep desire to change the world somehow?

A spark of hope in my dream of higher education still glimmered, and soon that spark was fanned into flame again. Music school wasn't exactly what I wanted—I wanted an American university education—but I told myself it was all right to change course since all other doors had obviously closed.

I researched a reputable music school in the state, but my heart fell when I read that the application process required an audition. I could practice, sure, but I had been without a piano teacher for more than a year and had only my memory to guide me in the audition preparation. As I was thinking about all of this, I realized I had just made a tremendous decision: I would apply to the music school. Wow. A complete change in course. Still, excitement began to grow as a plan developed, and optimism returned now that I had a new target in mind.

I decided to practice my favorite classical pieces: Mozart's Piano Sonata No. 16, and Bach's Prelude in C Major. Over and over, when I returned home from my night shift, I would stay up until well past midnight, playing the same songs, repeating each measure until my fingers knew instinctively where to go. Then I would play the entire song again, just to be sure. When I hesitated before a tricky part, I knew I slowed the tempo, and when I knew several measures well, I played faster. That would never do; I must play the music as written, evenly and according to the notations. Eventually, I could play the songs by memory, but I knew that excellent fingering was not enough. Music schools would look for *heart.* They would want to hear the decrescendo and the forte, the additional rest and the lilt of a light hand at the proper time. They would look for the music to speak to them or, rather, for *me* to speak to them through the music. I practiced and practiced, mentally reviewing the notes on my way to and from work, when I was cooking my breakfast and when I lay down at night to sleep. Surely, I had practiced enough; surely, I would score well. I had to. *I just had to.*

Audition Day arrived. I was ready. All the hours of practicing had provided me the extra measure of confidence I needed to play well enough to be accepted. Somehow, some way, I just knew this was the ticket to my college education. I just had to move through the steps. By the end of the evening, I would be making plans to move into the dorm rooms at the music school.

However, nervousness never completely leaves, even for the most seasoned professional. As I heard my name called and I walked slowly to the grand piano on stage in the music school auditorium, I was aware that one missed key, one fumbled fingering, one measure in disjointed timing, could dash all my hopes again. Apprehensive, I sat on the piano bench, my long black gown providing me at least the appearance of a professional musician. I moved my feet, shod in new black pumps, into position— left foot back, right foot on the pedals. I closed my eyes briefly, took a deep breath, and brought my hands down on the keys.

And I played. Oh, how I played! Every movement was precise, every note clear. My fingers raced to keep up with my thoughts, and I forced myself to play steadily, not altering the tempo unless the score had instructed me to slow for emphasis. I put everything I had into that audition, playing with my heart and soul. At the end, I let my hands rest briefly on the keys until the music faded away. I stood, bowed, and walked down the four steps to my seat. I was so pleased with my performance. The professors asked me to kindly wait in another room.

Surprised, I realized this must simply be standard protocol. They wanted to discuss my performance privately, and although I did not welcome additional delay, I smiled my agreement and left the room.

I waited an eternity. How odd that such a pivotal point in one's life is often left to the decision of others! But I had come this far; surely, I could wait twenty more minutes.

But only five minutes later, one of the female judges opened the door of the room where I had been waiting. She asked me to follow her back into the auditorium where I had auditioned. I smiled confidently; they were going to congratulate me on my acceptance into the music program, perhaps even offer me a scholarship!

The man, the dean of the piano school, spoke first and described to me how the scoring had taken place. Each judge had evaluated my performance based on specific criteria, using a point system to indicate an appropriate level of skill. The points had been tallied and averaged. I had received six out of ten possible points, and *eight* points were required for admission to the program. My application to the school had been denied.

I was devastated. The judge's voice sounded far away as he continued to describe the assessment process. But all I knew was I would not be attending classes there. All those hours of practice, all those late nights and skipped social engagements, all that discipline of not sleeping in but getting up early to practice before work—all that *time and effort*—wasted. I had absolutely nothing to show for all my sacrifice *again* except one more dream dashed to pieces. I realized the judges had stopped talking and were looking at me expectantly. I must have looked like a frightened deer; I simply could not comprehend that the audition was over and they were dismissing me. In a monotone, I asked if I could audition again. *Please, may I audition again?* I saw one judge look down and nod his head. *I could? When? Now? Next week?* Encouraged by that slight nod, I boldly asked what I could do to improve my performance, not understanding in the least why I had not scored a ten on the audition.

Surprisingly, I heard the female judge answer my question. "Hire a teacher, and practice." Scribbling on a scrap piece of paper, the judge wrote a name and number and handed the scrap to me. "Here is who we would recommend. She will help you get to where you want to go." I nodded my head, choked out a whispered "Thank you," gathered my music score and their paper evaluations, and rushed out the door before the tears could spill over. Oh, what was I to do now? I couldn't seem to catch my breath; I felt like I was drowning, and I wasn't even sure I could come up for air, or if I even wanted to. *After all my work!* Somehow, I had missed it again. I just wasn't cut out for this college thing. Uncle Robert back home in St. Vincent was right; he had told me life in America was harder than it was in St. Vincent. Many people had moved and tried to go after the American Dream only to come up empty and move back home to the island, to familiar people and familiar ways.

I didn't want that. I *knew* I didn't want that. Whatever I had missed, I was determined to find it. I would go home to St. Vincent, yes, *but I would be a visitor, not a resident!* This I knew in the depths of my heart. Something awaited me, something for me to do. I had come so close, so very close. Two points close! Two lousy points close!

I tossed the sheet music onto the backseat of my friend's car and went to get a cup of coffee on Main Street. I just wanted to think. What was different now from two hours ago? What had changed? I was still alive. Check. I still knew how to play the piano. Check. I still wanted to go to college. Double-check. And I still wanted to change the world. Triple check that one. Nothing about those things had changed.

So what *had* changed? One simple thought rose to my consciousness: The reality was that my piano playing simply lacked just two points of being accepted. I sipped my latte and continued thinking. I knew I was a good piano player. I was good enough to be a piano teacher, if I wanted to move in that direction, at least to teach beginning students. But something had changed in me as I had practiced for the audition: I had grown to enjoy the music—no, *I had grown to love the music*, to appreciate the genius of Mozart and Bach. I would hum the pieces to myself when I would do my chores, and I knew my practicing had become not only something to do to get me to where I wanted to go, but that the music itself had become a satisfaction, my fingers moving on the piano keys becoming a kind of medicine that soothed my soul, a benediction to the long days at work. I had discovered a love for music. The question then naturally formed in my head, "So, could that grow?"

A new revelation now blossomed in my mind. I simply wasn't as good as I thought I was. I wasn't as good as I *could* be. And I needed help.

With new resolve, coupled with an amazing realization that in such a short amount of time I could go from drowning to being back in the music pool swimming with more gusto than ever, I called the music teacher whose name was on the scrap of paper. Yes, she was available for an interview. When could I come?

I immediately rearranged my schedule to allow for five hours of practice every day. Yes, *five hours*. And I knew this time I wasn't practicing just to please a judge; I was practicing to master the music, to feel the composition, to express the heart of the score in a language understandable to others who listen not only with their ears but with their hearts. In six months, my piano teacher informed me I was ready, and I returned to the school auditorium with renewed confidence for another audition. I played flawlessly from my soul, capturing the notes and sending them into the air with bold confidence. I played not only for the judges, not only for my teacher, but for myself. For Mozart. For Bach.

This time I scored nine points, one entire point above the requirement!

Two weeks later, I was an official college student at the New York College of Music with a major in music education. My excitement on that first day of school was beyond words. I had done it! I had been accepted into college and I was on my way to learn—that in itself provided my basis for sheer joy as I entered the classroom. My dream was about to unfold day by day, assignment by assignment, and I couldn't wait for it to come true.

Two years went by. I worked hard at my assignments, never once taking for granted my attendance at the college. I approached every project with diligence and excellence; I read every text twice, once for an overview and the second for comprehension. I learned to ask myself questions, pretending I was the professor, and I found I was more than prepared for each day's lecture.

But then my academic skies began to darken; I heard rumors that the school was not meeting its financial obligations. Enrollment was declining and funds were running out. The administrators talked openly about cutting programs, and then certain teachers told us they would not be returning for the next term—that they had been let go.

As sad as I was to walk in on my favorite instructor packing up her desk, I felt a rising panic in me. "Is the school itself to close?" I choked out the question. Looking up from her packing, with tears in her eyes, the teacher nodded.

No! My heart thundered. *How could that be?* We students had received no notice, we still attended classes, and we still had homework assignments and exam dates. My teacher would talk no further about it, so I decided to talk to the dean the following afternoon. But I didn't have the opportunity. The next morning, when I went to my music theory class, the dean was in the room instead of the professor. She soberly informed us the school had filed for bankruptcy.

A hundred thoughts flashed through my mind in that moment. I had done my part, worked so hard. I had completed above and beyond what was required of me. What would become of me? What would become of all of us students? Would our school credit simply dissolve? Would they, in essence, just let us go too?

The dean was still talking. I stared at her blankly and steeled myself to hear her next words. Her face softened, and she explained that the school, though it could no longer afford to instruct us, would nonetheless do all it could to continue our education. To that end, the college had made arrangements for the entire current student body to be transferred to the music department at New York University, with all our current academic credits accepted.

The thoughts slowly halted as I let her words sink in. We had not been abandoned. *I* had not been abandoned. A plan was still set out before me. I just needed to go through the next step. Breathing steadily but not at all panicked, I went through the necessary paperwork that same afternoon, and I was officially transferred to the university. One week later, as I walked across my new campus, I realized I had an opportunity to change my major if I desired. I thought about that for only a moment. Remembering my original dream had been to eventually become a teacher of young children, I decided on the spot to change my major. Confidently, I marked my major as "elementary education" with a minor in music and art. In the most amazing way, I was exactly where I had always wanted to be: I was a student at an American university, pursuing a degree to become a teacher. I put down the pencil and took in the wonder of it all.

*****

I Can See Clearly Now

You could say that I eventually became a student at a top-level American university through the back door. But looking back, I realize I simply took advantage of every situation that presented itself. From asking questions to filling out applications to practicing the piano for hours on end, I trained myself not only in working hard but also in constantly reminding myself *to be willing* to work hard. With that mindset, I matched my actions to my desired destination and found I was prepared for the next step, even though sometimes that step was obscured. In the end, those qualities enabled me to graduate from an American university with the degree I had always wanted. I had received the best education possible, and I knew my dream had come true.

Reflection Questions

Do you value education? How has your education helped you to succeed?

_____

_____

_____

_____

In what areas would you like to have more education? What is stopping you from pursuing further education, whether formal or self-taught?

_____

_____

_____

_____

Sometimes things don't turn out how we want them at first, but in the end, everything works out for the best. When has this happened for you?

_____

_____

_____

_____

What have you learned from such situations? Have you come to trust yourself and the Universe as a result?

_____

_____

_____

_____

Chapter 5

Driving Dilemma

"Take the first step in faith. You don't have to see the whole staircase. Just take the first step."

— Martin Luther King, Jr.

I WILL NEVER FORGET the first time I sat behind the wheel of a car. The memory is strong and vivid, like it was yesterday.

Growing up in St. Vincent, I never had any need to drive. The island was so small we would walk most places and, if I did need to get somewhere by car, friends gladly drove me. When I moved to New York City, public transportation was easily available so, once again, I had no need to drive. While on the island, I'd simply been uninterested in driving. Once in New York, I caught on to how potentially scary driving could be.

Within a few years, I met and married a young man and we soon had children. With a five-year-old, an eleven-month-old, and my husband's fifteen-year-old nephew, Desmond, living with us at the time, our one-bedroom apartment in New York became quite crowded. Some days I felt like I couldn't turn around without bumping into somebody. I remember thinking that, even in St. Vincent with all the tourists, I had never felt overrun with people. But now, in my own home, I felt stifled, with not even a corner to call my own when I wanted to be alone.

My husband knew someone who lived in Norwalk, Connecticut, so one autumn weekend we took a Sunday drive there, falling in love with the amber gold and deep red maples that lined nearly every street. We decided right then and there to move, knowing we desperately wanted more elbow room. Why not drink in the lovely New England atmosphere while raising our children? Within two weeks, we found a lovely large house in Norwalk, well-suited to our growing family and located close enough to New York for my husband to commute to work.

Buying a house was an adventure in itself. Never had I known that purchasing something would require so much paperwork, so many telephone calls, and so much money! Naturally, those details consumed my days, along with tending to the children, the nephew, the meals, and the packing of a few boxes between changing diapers and doing some laundry. I hardly thought about transportation because I was just so grateful to get the money together to purchase the house. I didn't think to myself, "How will I go grocery shopping?" or anything like that. I wasn't looking ahead; I was dealing with the immediate present, my immediate reality. And, when you're the mother of a young child and a baby and you also work fulltime, immediate reality is what you deal with most of the time. I would think ahead only so far as moving into the house in Connecticut. I found myself beginning almost every sentence with, "After we move…." If the wastebasket was overflowing, I told my husband, "After we move, I'll have room for a wastebasket in every room." If the mail piled up on my desk, I would tell myself, "After we move, I'll sort the bills into folders in a file cabinet." I simply didn't think about anything past that one major event.

Moving Day arrived. For a full week after everything had been brought into our new home, I arranged the furniture, unpacked the boxes, and hung pictures on the walls. I mentally patted myself on the back, quite pleased with myself for tying up most of the loose ends from the move. The only thing left to do was to fill the empty shelves in the pantry and buy some milk, eggs, and meat for the near-empty refrigerator. We had been living on peanut-butter-and jelly sandwiches and apples since we had left the Bronx. I turned to get my purse to walk to the store down the street. But then I remembered that the store was not down the street. In fact, *no* store was within walking distance.

For the first time in my life, I was in a situation where public transportation or walking wasn't going to get me where I needed to go. Hmm…. *Why hadn't I thought of that before?* Like I said, during that time in my life, I lived mostly in the immediate present. I turned to my husband and asked him if he wanted to go on a date with me to buy some groceries. Perhaps his nephew would watch the children? Of course, I knew my husband would have to drive me, but I thought we could at least have some fun on the errand.

As it turned out, he had to drive me everywhere. To the grocery store. To the post office. To Bible Study. To the shoe repair place. Soon my husband was tired of being my chauffer because I always had a list of errands in my hand when he returned home from work each day. This would never do. Something had to change.

I was at a crossroads. I loved our new home, and I loved my family. But I would be restricted to the house and our immediate neighborhood if I continued to walk everywhere, and I would have to rely on my husband to take me most places. At the same time, I felt a rising anxiety at the prospect of learning how to drive. I followed my own reasoning to its logical conclusion: Learn to drive or be trapped. When my husband went off to work the first day after we moved to Norwalk, he drove himself to the train station, and I was struck hard by the stranded feeling that rose in my throat. I was unable to go anywhere, even in an emergency.

Anxiety is no easy thing to dismiss. I had seen the traffic in New York, and I knew of several people who had been killed in car accidents. I had often overheard drivers say that, although they trusted their own knowledge of their cars and their driving skills, they didn't trust the unexpected moves of other drivers. This is what really bothered me. To a certain degree, I was in control of my own life, and I prided myself on my independence. But once I climbed behind the wheel of a vehicle, I had no control over others' decisions. I also knew profoundly that the word "accident" meant just that. Sometimes brakes failed, occasionally someone was in a "blind spot," and often a driver was momentarily distracted by any number of things. Such distractions often led to tragedy, and I knew it. Our cars didn't have seatbelts back then, and I remembered a local fireman telling me that a person often survived the initial accident, even crashing through the windshield and being thrown from the car. It was the landing that caused death.

Plus, when I rode with my husband, I was amazed at everything I saw him do before he ever started the car: put in the key, check the rearview mirror, roll down the window to adjust the outside mirror, turn on the heater, and press on the brake. When we began to move, I noticed he had to coordinate pushing the accelerator with his foot, gripping the steering wheel with his hands, and glancing with his eyes at those mirrors and the road ahead. Occasionally, he pushed down the lever of the turn signal, and then when the winter rains came, he used the windshield wipers too. I didn't think I could ever do all that, and I didn't want to.

Still, I realized the final end: *I would be stranded if I didn't learn to drive, and I would gain tremendous freedom and independence if I did.* That did it. I knew from experience that freedom and independence won hands down every time over restriction and relying on others. If I refused to learn to drive—and it would be a downright refusal because the opportunity was in front of me—then I would grow to resent those who did drive, and that included the man I had married. And I didn't want that.

This all transpired in my head in only a few hours. Quickly I made the decision: I would learn to drive. *There! The hardest part is done.* I breathed a sigh of relief.

Once the decision was made, the thoughts came quickly, tumbling over each other. I would have to learn to drive soon because I had just been hired for a position at Cranbury Elementary School ten miles away! My husband had driven me to the interview, reminding me that the hiring manager, a member of the Board of Education, already knew me since he had owned the house we had just purchased. You would think I would have thought about transportation before I had applied for the position, but I didn't. Like I said, I lived in the immediate present in those days. Once we had relocated, my mind went on to the next major item on my mental checklist: Get an interview somewhere, anywhere, and secure employment. I never once thought about how I would *get to* a new job.

At this point, I knew my survival depended on learning to drive. I took a deep breath, picked up the phone book, and thumbed through the pages until I found, "Driving Schools." Wow. So many! Eventually, I saw an advertisement that read "for nervous drivers." Now that was the school for me! I called and set up an appointment for the end of the week. By the time the teacher arrived at our house on Friday afternoon to pick me up in the little Toyota Corolla with the huge sign on it that shouted to the world, "Student Driver," I had already worked myself into a nervous wreck. I had never, ever been behind the wheel of a car, even to sit without the engine on.

Mr. Elliott, my instructor, asked if I was ready to learn to drive. I nodded my head, thinking he would come in and we would talk about the rules of the road. Instead he motioned to the car. "Shall we get started?"

I was aghast. *Just like that? No prep talk? No pep talk? No discussion?* "Just get in?" My eyes widened.

"Yes." He opened the car door for me, smiling kindly. "Just get in."

Mute, I lowered myself into the driver's seat. Oh, everything looked so different from this perspective! My heart was pounding. I was actually sitting behind the wheel of a car in the driver's seat! Mr. Elliott closed my door, walked around the back of the car, and seated himself in the bucket seat next to mine.

Oh, no! I was absolutely petrified. *I have a passenger in the car, and I might kill us both!* I clenched my sweating hands together. I gritted my teeth. I was on the verge of tears. My teacher saw my nervousness and at once assured me that his side of the car was specially equipped with brakes and that he could override many of my driving decisions. He did his best to calm my nerves, but it was of little use. He went through the preliminary part of the driving instructions, naming the different parts of the dashboard as he pointed to them. I was barely breathing. He told me to put my foot on the brake and turn the key. *What? But this was my first lesson! We really weren't going to drive the car already?* Yes, we were. I clenched my lips together and stared straight ahead, pressing down on the accelerator like I had seen my husband do, and gripping the steering wheel like it was a lifeline thrown to a drowning swimmer. Suddenly, the term "white knuckles" seemed sensible and appropriate. The engine roared.

Mr. Elliott was patient. He smiled again and told me to "Let up on the gas," put my foot on the brake instead, and release the emergency brake. Thank God! I would have rammed us into the neighbor's parked car. He informed me that the vehicle would not move forward until I moved the gearshift handle from "Park." Calming down just a bit to listen to his words and then put them into action, I shifted the engine into "Drive." Carefully, at Mr. Elliott's instruction, I moved my foot and pressed the accelerator. *We were moving!*

That lesson was so long and I drove so slowly, all while my mind was buzzing. *Here I am, twenty-nine years old, and I'm driving like I'm ninety-two!* But when the forty-five minute lesson was over and I was at my front door once again, I realized I had actually driven a car. The thought was astounding. I was on my way to becoming a driver! The lesson had been difficult, actually harder that I had ever imagined. I knew it would have been easier if I had learned to drive at the traditional age of sixteen, when there was less fear and more teenage exuberance to overcome any hesitations. But I also knew that, no matter how nervous I was, I had to persevere.

Over the next several lessons, I loosened my grip on the steering wheel and slowly began to relax, if only a little. I simply *had* to learn to drive, no two ways about it. And now I was under a deadline of sorts. School was beginning in four weeks and, if I didn't learn to drive, I would have no way to get the children to school or myself to work.

I missed the deadline. Mr. Elliott thought, and I agreed, that I simply wasn't ready to pass the driving test yet. When school began in September, I was still taking driving lessons on Tuesday evenings and Saturday mornings, so I didn't yet have my license. This situation required me to pay a driver to first drop off our five-year-old daughter to school and then take me to work. I found these months to be especially difficult emotionally; I saw the hard-earned money I was receiving from my new job leave as quickly as it came in because I had to pay someone else to take me and our daughter where we needed to go. On the weekends, Mr. Elliott would pick me up for my lesson and we would drive to the beach. That gave me plenty of practice in navigating both the freeways and the traffic. One day while I glanced at the lovely deep green of the Atlantic Ocean, I realized I was simultaneously immersed in learning the ropes for my new job as well as studying and practicing for my driver's license exam. No wonder I was having a hard time—my mind whirred with all that I had to learn at once. The mental strain occasionally revealed itself in a lack of sleep and subsequent irritation at my family. At the least, I was often preoccupied at home, mentally reviewing my notes, and I usually caught up on sleep on Sunday afternoons when the children went with their dad to the park. One way I coped was to tell myself I was only doing what had to be done and that this entire situation was temporary. Although I never was completely comfortable, I nonetheless eventually loosened my grip on the steering wheel during those twice-weekly driving lessons.

By November, Mr. Elliott finally said I was ready to take the exam. I was so nervous, I was sure I would fail. Without my driving instructor beside me, I felt like a beginning driver again, and I thought my nervousness would cause me to forget vital steps or that I would simply not be concentrating enough to judge the speed of an oncoming car when making a left turn. For a moment, the old fear rose up in me that I was responsible for two lives in this little Toyota. But then I felt the fear melt into sober awareness. Yes, I *was* responsible for navigating this huge, heavy piece of equipment safely. I *was* always to remember that driving was a privilege, and I *was* to do all in my power to navigate the residential roads and public highways with great caution. But I also realized *I was prepared.* I had trained well for this appointment, and Mr. Elliott was an excellent teacher. I knew I was especially weak in the area of parallel parking. But with firm resolution, I told myself if I failed in any regard, I would simply study, practice more, and come at it again.

To my astonishment, I passed both the written test and the behind-the-wheel exam the first time! I was ecstatic! My entire world suddenly shifted as I realized I could drive all by myself if I wanted. I was once again the master of my own time and space. The feeling of accomplishment was incredible, especially after all the stress of the preceding months. Confidence rose in me as I posed for my driver's license picture. As I walked back to Mr. Elliott, waiting for me in the parking lot, I knew I had taken a significant step toward making my life easier. I was so relieved to know I could be more independent and not have to rely on others.

But I had one more hurdle to overcome: The little Toyota Corolla from the driving school had an automatic transmission; the Datsun B210 my husband and I owned had a standard transmission, commonly known as a stick shift. I hired Mr. Elliott for a few more lessons. I found it no easy task to maneuver my feet at two different positions and pressures, move a stick while listening to the whine of the engine rev up and, at the same time, watch the road and mirrors and steer the car. The first time driving down the street from our house, I felt the familiar symptoms of sweaty palms and clenched teeth. But this time, I knew I *could* learn. I knew I *would* learn. Even with all the cars honking when I forgot to shift gears, I took a deep breath, went through all the steps carefully, and shifted properly. Done!

Naturally, our schedule at home changed once I received my license. Being a working mother is usually stressful anyway, but now I knew this change would be simply one more challenge to navigate. And so every weekday morning I would awaken, dress myself and the children, prepare breakfast for the family, drive my husband to the bus stop, drop the girls off at the babysitter's, and then go to work. In the late afternoon, I would reverse the process, picking up my husband later in the evening. We owned only one car, and sometimes, we found it difficult to coordinate our schedules, but we made it work.

*****

I Can See Clearly Now

Learning to drive was a major accomplishment for me. When I first started, I never imagined I would become the relaxed and confident driver I am today. The entire experience proved to me again that I can do anything I put my mind to. The struggles I've had have only made me stronger! I still do not like driving long distances, more than thirty minutes. And I do not drive on highways, staying only on local residential streets. And I will definitely not drive anywhere in New York City. To this day I prefer to drive all the way around a block to find a different parking space rather than parallel park. I realize I could do all of that if I had to and wanted to, but I choose not to, and I'm okay with that.

Our daughters don't have the fear about driving that I had. They each learned how to drive when they were sixteen, and they have no problem driving in city traffic. Like I said, I think the excitement of youth may have something to do with that. By the time I started driving, I was well into adulthood, and my experience prompted the profound awareness of what I was doing and what could happen if I was careless. Youth rarely has that perspective. Despite still having minor anxiety when I drive, I am far from the twenty-nine-year-old woman who gripped the steering wheel in terror. Today, I steer with confidence, looking in the mirrors briefly now and then to see what is behind me, and confidently looking forward, knowing anything is possible in life. The motions of looking back and looking ahead remind me of my journey, and I hear the words again in my heart. *No matter what happens, I'll never, ever give up.*

Reflection Questions

What do you fear? On a separate piece of paper, write down all your fears. Go over each one and write one way you can combat each fear.

Now on another piece of paper, make a list of positive affirmations that help combat those fears. (For example, if you have a fear of being alone, write: I am happy and safe in my home.)

Burn the piece of paper with your fears on it. Watch it burn and think about releasing your fears.

Each day, do something you're afraid of. Take baby steps. Celebrate your successes.

Seek others who have overcome the fears you have. Talk with them and ask for their support.

Chapter 6

I Will Survive

"Nothing in the world can take the place of persistence. Talent will not: nothing is more common than unsuccessful men with talent. Genius will not: unrewarded genius is almost a proverb. Education alone will not: the world is full of educated derelicts. Persistence and determination alone are omnipotent."

— Calvin Coolidge

MY WORST NIGHTMARE happened right in front of my eyes and I never saw it coming. It happened when my husband and I had been married for well over a decade, my hands were full of mothering three children under the age of ten, and I was working full time. I taught fourth grade at the elementary school across town, and I loved it. Life can be dull sometimes as an adult, but for ten-year-old kids, life is just beginning.

They're old enough to see the glimmers of adulthood down the road but young enough to still laugh and play, flashing a triumphant smile when they've worked a long division problem correctly. And I loved their curiosity. But working at the school as well as parenting our own children and managing our household was tiring and, like most working mothers, I found it imperative to maintain a strict schedule to make everything work.

Most mornings, I would turn off the alarm at 5:30 a.m. and get myself ready for the day except for my shoes—I could move faster around the house in my slippers! I would wake the girls and dress the toddler. Then it was downstairs for breakfast, a quick clean-up, and then out the door with backpacks on and lunches in hand. I took the older girls to their school and then dropped off the youngest at the babysitter's before I headed for work. Once I walked into the classroom, it was writing lesson plans, checking homework assignments, and introducing new skills—I especially enjoyed our science experiments. A few teachers' meetings here and there, a stack of papers to take home to grade after the girls were in bed, and I was soon back in the car. Pick up the girls, run a few errands, and then home to make dinner. Our days were full.

By the time the children were asleep, all I wanted to do was go to sleep myself, but I had those papers to correct and the next day's lessons to review. I would make myself a cup of tea and head to my desk for a few hours, telling myself I was setting a good example for our daughters—women could pursue their dreams and have a family too. You just had to be organized and disciplined and manage your time well.

Everything was great, or so I thought.

Life has its ups and downs for everyone, of course, but I had always looked at the downs as temporary. My husband was out of work and my teaching salary was not enough to cover our expenses, especially since I wasn't paid during the summer months. I told myself we would get through this tough time of tight finances. My primary focus was to look after the children, teach, and maintain an upbeat attitude. But tension was rising between my husband and me. He began leaving the house during the day, telling me he was looking for a job, but then not coming home at night. Naturally, I worried about him, thinking he had been hurt in an accident; this was back in the days before cellphones. When he sauntered in one morning after being gone for two days, I held my tongue until after I had returned home from work later that afternoon. Then it was time for a direct conversation.

"Where have you been?" I demanded. His casual, evasive answer provoked me even more, and soon we were engaged in a fierce argument. I demanded to know where he had lived for two days, but he refused to tell me, saying he didn't need to answer to me and he surely didn't need another mother.

I was shaken. We had been so close at one time, pledging to each other our lives. We had three beautiful, innocent girls—Debbie, Malene, and Nneka—with a future in front of them. Neither my husband nor I had grown up with two parents in the home, so we had determined early on not to repeat the cycle of a broken marriage.

Yet something was very wrong. We became cordial to one another only when our daughters were around, and harsh and cold when they were not. I felt caught between a child's lighthearted world of innocent grins and a confused adult world of growing anxiety.

My low self-esteem did not help the tension. I was sixty pounds overweight and desperately wanted to believe my husband loved my heart and my weight didn't bother him. But, even if that were true, it bothered *me*, so I pummeled myself inwardly every time I put on a pair of jeans and struggled to zip and button them. I concentrated on applying makeup and wearing trendy earrings, hoping others would concentrate on looking at my face, and I consciously put on a smile whenever I was out of the house, doing all I knew to convince others to remember my optimistic personality and forget my obvious lack of self-control when it came to food. I struggled between feeling ugly on the outside and wanting desperately to be thought beautiful on the inside.

My weight wasn't the only wedge between my husband and me, of course, but it was an obvious one, so I told myself all would be well if I just lost weight. Looking back, I recognize this as one of my first signs of denial that our relationship was unhealthy. My desire to lose weight, on the surface, was based on a noble desire to please him. But, actually, it was a twisted attempt to justify his increasingly cruel comments about my appearance. But I didn't know that then. He was my husband, I was his wife, we had three children, and we were on our way to having a lovely life. Weren't we?

No, we weren't.

On a sunny Connecticut spring morning, my husband told me to come into the family room. Drying my hands on a dish towel, I followed him and stood silently while he turned around to face me.

"I want a divorce."

I blinked. I stopped drying my hands and stared at him in disbelief. I stuttered. "Wh-wh-what?"

He refused to discuss the matter, saying he would be packing his clothes and leaving right away. He said he didn't love me and he wanted to live on his own. I knew we had been going through a particularly difficult time lately, but I had never imagined he would leave. I was stunned.

Still holding the dish towel, his words traveling now from my ears to my heart, I began to sway. Surely, this wasn't happening! Surely, I had misunderstood. I was nauseous. Perhaps he wanted a few weeks just for some space, to think things over. In a heartbeat, every negative emotion tumbled over me like I had been thrown overboard from a raft, the rapids pushing me down, down, causing me to hit the rocks on the river bottom while I desperately tried to come up for air. Fear, failure, doubt, and panic—especially panic— rose up one by one and then pushed me back down to that breathless darkness.

He turned. I knew instinctively he was going upstairs to pack. *No! He can't leave!* I threw the dishtowel on the floor, followed him to the bedroom, and pulled at his sleeve, begging him to stay, to reconsider his decision. I told him we would go to marriage counseling, that we would get help. He stopped momentarily, looked at me, and then shook his head. His words of a few moments before were now sinking in; a picture flashed in my mind of a broken family. He was really leaving, and I would really be raising the girls alone. Yes, I had a job, but that job paid very little, not nearly enough to pay all our bills. We had used the last of the money in our savings account to pay the car insurance the previous week. I had nothing to fall back on. And I had only twenty dollars in my wallet. He was leaving immediately and, if he did, the last opportunity for us to talk this out would leave with him. My dream of a perfect family was unraveling thread by thread, right in front of my eyes, and I felt powerless to stop it. He was deserting us! Our children would grow up fatherless—something I had desperately wanted to avoid since I had grown up without a father. My parents had divorced when I was five and my father had deserted us, moving to Trinidad. I did not want the same pain for my girls that I had experienced. And I was being left alone, without a companion, partner, or lover. All alone. How could that be? How could that happen? My begging turned to pleading. Desperation rose in my voice.

"Please, don't leave!" My eyes welled with tears. Again I begged him to stay, pleading for our marriage, for our girls, for our future. And I pled for my dreams, for my life, for my sanity. Suddenly, I knew I didn't care that he was unemployed, that he had called me names because of my weight, that he had neglected the children for weeks on end, and that he had lied repeatedly to me. Our entire twelve-year marriage was at stake, and I didn't care what kind of marriage it was; any kind of marriage was still a marriage, and I was desperately and entirely terrified of raising three children all by myself.

I fell to my knees in front of him. Like a starved beggar devoid of every shred of self-respect, I was willing to accept any crumbs of hope my husband might offer. He didn't have to give me a full meal, didn't have to provide even a small crust of bread. Just some crumbs, just a few itty-bitty crumbs. I was groveling, and I knew it. But I was willing to take the crumbs over a future of loneliness, fatherless children, and broken dreams. He put a pair of shoes in a duffle bag.

I promised to lose weight. Yes, that was the answer—if I lost weight, he would stay, wouldn't he? *Wouldn't he?* My mind scrambled for more things I could do to persuade him to stay. He tossed some shirts into the bag. "I'll be quiet during the day, when you're sleeping, and I'll make sure to have dinner on the table at five every night, and I won't ask you where you've been when you come home in the morning after being gone all night." Yes, I'll do that. And I'll do more. Anything. *I'll do anything!* He zipped the bag shut.

He left anyway, of course. He refused to admit any wrongdoing in our marriage, refused to talk about it, and refused to reconsider his decision. His mind was made up, and he gave me neither time nor opportunity to react in any other way than thunderstruck panic. In thirty minutes, he was gone, not even saying goodbye to the children. The toddler was crying because of the shouting, the five-year-old woke from her nap and came downstairs rubbing her eyes, and the ten-year-old stood mutely, looking at the door that had slammed behind her father as he had walked out, with a look of terror on her face. My life was absolutely decimated, and I had children to tend to.

My husband never returned, not even for a night. He had no interest in any attempt at reconciliation, and his abrupt departure shook me to my bones. I was completely shattered. For the next three days, I was unable to halt the tears. I cried when I awakened in the night, hoping desperately that the nightmare was not real. I cried when I took a shower, the pounding water drowning out my heaving sobs. I cried when I stirred the grits, when I set down the bowls—minus one now—when I washed the spoons, my tears falling into the dirty dishwater. Soon, my eyes were nearly swollen shut with constant crying. Everything had fallen apart. Absolutely everything. I would have almost welcomed news of his death from a car accident, grieving over something beyond our control. But this! *This we could have worked out.* This grief—this overwhelming, unbearable, crushing-my-gut-to-the-point-where-I-can-hardly-breathe kind of grief—was relentless, hammering, and slicing. Not only had I lost a husband and our children their father, but *I had been rejected.* This pain hurt almost more than his leaving. My fragile self-esteem exploded into smithereens. For years, he had rejected me privately—I was accustomed to that—but finding out within days that he had rejected me in favor of someone else, someone *thin* who had told me she was my friend, was a public way of shouting to the world I was not good enough. Not good enough to hold on to a man. Not good enough to hold on to my marriage. Not good enough to hold my family together. I was now not only shattered, my very being shaken with profound pain; I was also devastated with unbearable shame.

The moments crawled by on that April morning after the slamming of the front door until I slowly came to my senses. I picked up crying Daughter Number Three, cuddled Daughter Number Two, and drew into my embrace our shaking firstborn. Fighting hard to quiet my own pounding heart, I knew my first step was to regroup mentally. Soon I made arrangements with a neighbor for immediate childcare for an hour, pushed a handful of tissues into my jacket pocket, and headed by foot to the beach a half-mile away, tears streaming down my face. The intensity of that painful walk seared itself into my soul.

I returned around five o'clock with a firm resolve to take my life moment by moment from that point forward. I had three children to care for, the eldest being devastatingly aware of what had just happened. Blessedly, the younger children did not realize at the time the destruction of our family. I moved through what needed to be done: making phone calls, blotting my tears, making decisions, and continually fighting rising terror.

And dealing with anger. Oh, how I was angry. Defense for our young daughters rose up in me like never before. He could do this to me; okay, I got it. I was an adult. But break the trust of our *children*? Break their hearts? Uh-uh, buddy. Not on my watch. The Mama Bear came out in me in spades, and I determined to be the best mother—and father—any child could have. I would lavish them with love and attention and, by golly, I would provide for them, one way or another.

During that walk on the beach, while my bare feet pounded the sand and the blood pounded my temples, when I momentarily felt the wind knocked out of me, I had realized weirdly that I was still breathing after all and that I had a life to live. The question was: How was I to do that? The way I saw it, I had two choices: I could allow myself to drown, or force myself to swim. Looking at the ocean, vast and calm, yet mighty and powerful, the choice was clear. I would swim. Mentally dusting off the sorrow in my heart and physically wiping away the tears that fell from my eyes, I began to plan.

I had been a member of a weight-loss support group, but now I would attend with a new fervor. I *would* stick to the plan; I *would* choose healthy foods to eat and, with God's help, I *would* lose weight. And I did.

My salary at my new job was only $18,000 a year—not nearly enough to support me and three children with adequate food and shelter. We were in survival mode, to be sure. Although I had remained living in our house after my husband left, being a homeowner was no easy responsibility. The first year of being a single parent, I had to replace the roof and the septic tank. Often I had no oil for the oil tank in the house.

I had considered moving, of course. Perhaps renting would be more stable, with fewer unexpected expenses. But that idea came and went—my children needed stability now more than ever, and I determined that house repairs would be less traumatic than uprooting them from familiar surroundings. Their lives had already been turned upside down in more ways than I could count. Yet the dilemma remained of paying for the repairs in addition to meeting the monthly obligations with my meager earnings. So, while the girls were at camp, I took a summer job teaching macramé in adult education centers to make ends meet.

In the meantime, I discovered every consignment store and tag sale in the area so I could clothe my children. And, slowly—ever so slowly—I began to realize our lives were developing a rhythm, a calm routine of living together despite our broken hearts. And those broken hearts were beginning to mend somewhat. I realized I didn't have it in me to be both mother and father to our three children; I could only be the best mother I could possibly be. And now I saw more clearly how I had allowed deception to creep into our marriage and chosen to deny the signs of an unhealthy relationship. For the next several years, with much thought and prayer, I changed the way I thought about myself. I was no longer someone to be belittled. And I was no longer someone whom I despised. I was someone who was able to cope with day-to-day life, confident in my abilities to provide for my girls, and secure in my own personhood. I was of value because I was, simply, *someone of value.* I knew no one—*no* one—could ever again take that knowledge away from me. That confidence spilled over onto my girls, especially my oldest, and I saw my firstborn push off her young panic and replace it with a desire to help me wherever and whenever she could. We pulled together in those early months to tend to the younger children, to get dinner on the table, and to read a bedtime story to the five-year-old. Now she and I had settled into a new reality, one where we knew we were capable of designing our own attitudes and destinies to a degree, and we knew we were going to be all right. It wasn't long before she relaxed into our new routine and became a child again, secure in knowing I would never leave her.

During those first horrible months, with little money in our checking account, I insisted my ex-husband fulfil his financial obligation to our children. He promised to support them monthly, and I was hopeful that at least this area was settled. But the character traits I had been unwilling to see when we were married were now making themselves glaringly obvious. Money rarely came our way, and after a few months, I learned not to count on it. By court mandate, his wages were to be garnished when he did eventually return to work, but that proved only to be temporary income from him. During a court hearing for child support, the judge ordered him to pay child care arrearage of $1,000 immediately. He could not come up with that amount so the judge ordered him to be put in jail until it was paid. His friend gave him the money immediately and, by the end of the day, he was out of jail. That would be the last financial support I would receive from him for twenty years.

Allowing him to see the children was a different matter. Even if we were no longer husband and wife, we were still father and mother to three girls. I determined to do everything possible to foster a healthy relationship between them and their dad. He lived less than an hour away, so I was hopeful we could work out arrangements. At first, he did see the children—an afternoon at the park here, an evening at the movies there. But his visits became shorter and shorter, dwindling from several hours every few weeks to ten minutes every few months, just enough time for the girls to voice the same questions I had in my heart: *Why does he leave so soon, Mommy? Doesn't he love us?*

I had no answers. Soon his visits stopped altogether.

The divorce stands out in my mind as one of the most difficult times of my life. During my marriage, I was overweight, had no self-esteem, and became completely dependent on someone else for my emotional wellbeing. During the weeks after signing the divorce documents, I thought the hopelessness, sadness, and despair would never end. I was continually on guard lest those feelings swallow me whole. But somewhere, down deep in my being in the darkest of moments, something flickered. *I did not want to give up.* I could not give up; I had three young lives to care for. Sheer determination carried me through those difficult and exhausting months. I was often discouraged and wanted to give up. But, in the end, I came to see I had an innate power of persistence, something I realized is in all of us, something put there for our very survival. Desperation over my situation gradually gave way to gratitude for that instinct, and I came to realize persistence and prayer paired well together.

Every dollar was stretched until it was so threadbare I could see through it. A precious friend gave us her daughter's outgrown clothes, and another friend put oil in our oil tank one winter without wanting repayment. Still another friend lent me her car until I could afford to purchase one, and yet another friend paid my car insurance so I could drive to work. These were my everyday miracles, and I was so thankful. I often wondered why my husband's family never offered to buy anything for the girls, but I never asked for their help. And I didn't ask my family for help either; I knew they had their own problems and struggles. After a while, I ceased even thinking about their lack of help. I discovered I could figure out myself what needed to be done every step of the way, and then I would just do it. I became handy around the house and, although I made many mistakes, I nonetheless painted walls, fixed leaky faucets, repaired broken cabinet doors, and mowed lawns. When a maintenance problem arose, I asked around, read about it in the library, and solved the problem myself. I don't know how I did it, but I did it. *I did it!* During those times of great uncertainty, those periods of intense loneliness, and those hours of hard work, one sentence repeatedly sounded in my mind: *I will survive!* A current song by Gloria Gaynor with that phrase as its title became my daily theme and constant anchor.

I don't think the feelings of wanting to be loved and cared for ever go away, no matter how old we are. My girls, though now emotionally healthy, still missed the influence of a father, and I truly missed having a loving partner. I often wondered if I would ever find a man who would love not only me but my three children. I knew that would be something tremendous to ask of any man, to step into the role of father.

But it happened. Oh, gloriously, it happened. One day, a fine-looking gentleman walked up to me at a birthday party and introduced himself. I found his smile immediately assuring, and his unassuming, humble demeanor deeply attractive. Soon, we were seeing each other regularly, and instead of being threatened by my now-strong, no-nonsense personality, he told me he liked my independence and determination—that I was special indeed and a rare find. After a month of nearly-nightly phone calls, I invited him to meet my daughters. They loved him from that first dinner together. Amazingly, to me, he welcomed the girls as his own, and I knew I had found a life partner.

Before long, after we had become accustomed to being together as a family and comfortable with our new life, I began to think about returning to school to advance my education. I loved teaching, but I also loved variety, and I didn't want to be an elementary schoolteacher forever. I also knew that, in the field of education, more degrees equated to earning more money. After talking with my life partner and the children, I arranged our schedules and finances to accommodate a babysitter, and I returned to college, eventually earning a master's degree in counseling and, later, a doctorate in administration from Columbia University.

In the meantime, my daughters grew up beautifully. My dreams for them came true when they all graduated from college and, today, they are independent, successful women.

*****

I Can See Clearly Now

As horrific as the divorce was at the time, I can see now that it not only marked the end of my marriage, but the end of a decade of depending on someone undependable. Unwittingly, I had allowed our marriage to become emotionally unhealthy. My life revolved around my husband to such an extent that I failed to see the signs that I was becoming increasingly codependent, enabling him to continue not to work after two full years of unemployment. After the divorce, when I began slowly but surely to recover, I recognized how dangerously unhealthy I had become. Yes, I had contributed my own harsh accusations in our marriage, but most of that came out of frustration, ignorance, and pain. Once he had gone and I was left to make my own decisions, I discovered I had an inner strength I never knew I had. I read books, I talked with people, and I researched my options. When the ignorance began to melt into knowledge, the panic subsided, and I began to breathe again. Soon a plan began to form in my mind and I was able to draw strength to put that plan into action for a healthy future. In fact, I used two predominant skills I had learned when I was twelve years old: creativity and problem-solving.

Hindsight always helps put things in the proper perspective.

Reflection Questions

When has someone you loved or trusted betrayed you? How did it make you feel?

_____

_____

_____

_____

What coping skills did you learn in that situation?

_____

_____

_____

_____

Looking back, what role might you have played that negatively contributed to the situation?

_____

_____

_____

_____

Have you applied what you learned from this situation to future relationships in your life? What has been the result?

_____

_____

_____

_____

Chapter 7

Taking a Stand

"The real tragedy of life is not that each of us doesn't have enough strengths; it's that we fail to use the ones we have. Benjamin Franklin called wasted strengths 'sundials in the shade.'"

— Author Unknown

TEACHING FOURTH GRADE for fifteen years was fulfilling. I loved the inquisitiveness of the young children, but I also knew I didn't want to stay in that position my entire career. So, wanting to increase my income and thriving on challenge, I surveyed my options and concluded, *What could be more challenging than being around teenagers?* I set my sights on becoming employed at a high school. Just the thought of eventually being around more mature students watered the seed of motivation in me, so I soon reenrolled in college to earn the necessary certification to become a guidance counselor.

After I secured a position as a counselor at the local high school, I was officially rubbing shoulders with young adults poised to finish their basic studies and jump off into adult lives of their own. American society was changing quickly, and these young people would be right in the thick of it. How exciting for them! I enjoyed my new surroundings and took great pleasure in encouraging students to take certain classes, pointing them more accurately in the direction of a productive and satisfying future. The local superintendent was new to the district, so he decided to interview every teacher. During our visit, he encouraged me to consider a degree in administration since the school district would have an opening in that role at the high school in a few years and my high energy and creativity would be an asset there. I remember smiling and giving him my thanks. When the office door closed behind him, I pondered his remarks for a few moments.

Being around the faculty at the high school had, indeed, given me ideas for my future. Life had taught me that successful learning best takes place when the student and the teacher have the parents' support so all three roles blend and overlap. I had been watching closely how the administration at my school had handled these three roles, and I could feel ideas brewing in my mind. I began to imagine how, like a pilot seeing an entire town within a state from his plane, I could see an entire school within a community from my perspective. Eventually, I came to believe I could better help students overall by becoming an administrator. This aim, my most ambitious yet, would require yet another degree. But the decision process was easier this time because I had become practiced in working for the future. So I soon became a student again and earned a doctorate from Columbia University.

Now I was ready. I had the education. I had the experience. I had the desire. And I had the resume. I mean, I *had* the resume. At every job, in every position, I had reference letters with excellent reviews about my performance. In every college class, with every assignment, I had meticulously completed my work, training myself in excellence. I was well acquainted with preparing schedules, staying within a budget, preparing an agenda, and running a meeting. And I was extremely skilled at negotiating problems to arrive at acceptable solutions. When I walked across the stage to receive my doctorate diploma, I knew that I was well prepared to administrate in any high school in the country. I could hardly wait to apply for a position.

I didn't wait long. A position for vice principal opened at the very school in which I wanted to work. I applied for the job and soon received a call for an interview. Buoyant and expectant, I knew I was ready to answer any question I might be asked. That morning, I mentally reviewed my responses to possible scenarios as I drove to the interview. The superintendent—the same one who had encouraged me to further my education—met me at the door and ushered me into his office. For over an hour, he described my responsibilities and asked me what I would do in particular situations. He explained the district's policies and the school's mission statement. He asked detailed questions about my resume and my work as a guidance counselor. None of this was new to me, so I answered each question directly and confidently. At the interview's conclusion, he smiled warmly, thanked me for my application, and assured me I was well qualified for the position.

For the next two weeks, I imagined myself at my new desk. I knew the high school well, so I was already mentally making notes of which programs I would bring in and which ones I would eliminate. I already knew several of the teachers, and I thought I could give valuable insight to them about how to better their effectiveness in the classroom. I had kept up with advancements in my field, and I had some solid ideas about how we could raise the school's SAT scores.

Then I received a phone call from the superintendent's secretary, informing me that the district had hired someone else.

I was shocked—stunned really. The job had been perfect for me, and I had been perfect for the job. The news was even more bewildering because of my previous conversation with the superintendent years earlier when he had recommended I pursue this career path. He had known at the time that I had applied to several positions at the elementary level, but my lack of administrative experience in those days disqualified me from those jobs. So, at his suggestion and with the assumption that I would be a good fit for future positions, I had gone back to school. Now, here I was, qualified and confident, and I had been turned down. None of it made sense. I had all the necessary credentials now, *plus* the required experience. And I was well known to the superintendent and other professionals in the district. I felt not only disappointed but also confused.

Then I heard that the superintendent had given the high school position to a man with credentials far inferior to mine. A white man.

My disappointment gave way to a feeling of betrayal. I am an African-American woman, and it certainly appeared to me that this was a clear case of discrimination.

I mentally examined the situation. Considering the obvious difference in credentials between the other applicant and myself, I couldn't help but wonder if my race and gender were factors in the final decision. Certainly, I felt I was being denied an opportunity I deserved. I examined the matter from every angle, and the entire situation appeared plainly unjust and unfair. I had worked hard—*very* hard—and to be denied a position on any other basis than my qualifications was a hard blow. My thoughts turned to another direction.

Was this worth a fight? Racial issues had always been in the news to some extent, but we were long past the days of Martin Luther King, Jr. Some areas of the United States embraced progressive thought, and employees in most workplaces were treated equally. I knew, however, that in many other areas of the country, racial equality was nonexistent. To my mind, the only way prejudice would be overcome is by person-to-person contact, with the law of the United States Constitution backing it up. Professionally, I had worked hard and done the right thing—played by the rules, educated myself, and gained experience. Courtesy and respect were my hallmarks. If I decided to address this private matter in an open and public legal setting, would it damage my reputation? If I lost, would I be able to work in the district ever again?

But if I won? *If I won!* If I won, wouldn't that send a message not only to the school district officials, but to the students, parents, and community—the three places I hoped to impact—that prejudice would not be tolerated in any form within the school? Wouldn't the national conversation about race be addressed on the home-front? Talked about at the dinner table? Wasn't this what we, the African-American population, wanted?

I decided to take the next step and simply find out about my legal rights. I consulted an attorney who specialized in discrimination. After our two-hour meeting, he assured me he had never seen such a blatant case of discrimination. I considered my options. This would be new territory for me, and I was not a little uneasy. In fact, I was outright scared. Who knew where such a decision could lead? But if I *didn't* address the situation, would I be joining the thousands of other black people who never spoke up, allowing prejudice to continue? I made my decision. With my head up and my voice firm, I told the lawyer I would like to file a lawsuit against the local board of education and the superintendent.

Within days, my attorney wrote to the superintendent to inform him of our intention to pursue the matter further if the injustice wasn't corrected. The letter read, in part, "From everything I am able to discern in the course of my investigation of this matter, Dr. Barnett is a victim of racial and gender discrimination, and the action of the Board of Education is in clear violation of both federal and state discrimination laws."

And then we waited.

Within days, we heard from the superintendent; he wished to discuss the matter. Eventually, after four weeks and several consultations between my attorney and the superintendent, I was offered the position of assistant principal at a middle school. I declined the job, not out of spite, but because it wasn't the position for which I had applied. I did not want to administrate at a middle school; I wanted to use my skills and abilities at the high school to which I had applied. That would settle the dispute fairly, to my way of thinking.

A few days later, I received a call telling me to report to work at the high school to which I had applied. I was elated! I had won the fight!

But I was not naïve. Settling the incident legally resulted in my getting the position I wanted—and deserved—but that would not pave the way for smooth relationships once I began to work at the school. Understandably, some of the faculty did not want me there because I had caused the school and the district great embarrassment. On my first day of work, I told myself I might be walking into a hornet's nest so I had better prepare to get stung.

And that's just what happened.

The principal obviously did not want me there, greeting me with barely a nod when I walked behind the counter to my new office. He gave me my assignments and that was it—no explanations, no showing me around the school, nothing. The other assistants and secretaries spoke to me only when I asked specific questions. No "Good mornings," no offers to show me the school schedule, no inclusion in office chatter. To be sure, I hadn't expected a warm welcome, but I was shocked nonetheless by the ice-cold reception I received. I forced myself to smile and be polite as I asked question after question. I learned later that they considered me a militant.

When I looked at the administrative assignments the principal had given me, I wondered if he was intentionally hoping I would fail. He had assigned me two-thirds of all the responsibilities, a heavier load than the other two experienced assistant principals combined. Now that I was employed at the school, I knew I was facing my first interpersonal challenge of inequality and I would be wise to handle it personally and not legally. After a few moments of considering my next move, I decided to say nothing but simply to accomplish the work. I went to my office, looked at the list of responsibilities analytically, and then broke down the many duties into bite-size pieces. Soon I had papers in separate file folders, to-do lists divided into specific categories, and several meetings scheduled on the calendar.

The open rejection hurt worse than I could have imagined. In the late afternoons, after I had completed phone calls, had checked off items on my list, and had locked my office door to go home for the night, I would wonder if I had done the right thing to challenge the initial hiring decision. Although I was weary from putting in a full day of work, I was also emotionally tired from putting so much energy into every sentence I spoke, being careful of the intonation in my voice, and purposely deciding to ignore stares from the faculty. I felt like I was working two jobs at the same time, and I was exhausted. I would mull over the larger picture of racial inequality and wonder if my legal stand had helped or hindered the cause. To think that our country had come so far in making every citizen equal under the law, only to have people in the community not practice that equality, made me desperately want to change that social landscape. Yet I wondered if I had it in me to confront daily my coworkers' thinly-veiled hostility and the occasional outright rudeness from parents.

Every time I went over the situation in my mind, I came to the same conclusion: I never could have let the discrimination stand. I felt just like the leaders who broke down walls in the civil rights days to get justice and, although this was 1992, a time long past the civil rights movement, I realized that years of prejudice seemed to be ingrained in some people, regardless of the law, and that prejudice went two ways. Many of my friends and family had wondered why I had pursued litigation in order to get my job. They didn't know why I even wanted to work in a school that was 99.9 percent white. But I never understood why anybody should be treated differently simply because of the color of their skin. I wanted to contribute to changing that way of thinking and, if I could remain strong but not unkind, perhaps I could make some inroads at the school for the next African-American employee.

My personal mission became simple: to persuade my coworkers that I was an American just like they were. I had hopes and dreams too, and I was willing to work for them like anybody else. I had a family, I paid my bills, and I went to church just like they did. So, although it was the hardest thing I had ever done, I pushed open the doors of the school every morning with fresh determination to be pleasant and professional. And I would pray, "God, you walk in front of me and I will walk behind you."

Not all the people at the school ostracized me, but most did. At first, the only people at the school who welcomed me were the custodians, who were also black. They supported me because they were proud that I had fought for my position. They felt I represented them. I was also blessed with a magnificent secretary who became not only my right-hand person but also my friend. Her support and encouragement kept me going in those early days.

During this time, I prayed a great deal and began a serious spiritual journey, concentrating on my own personal growth. I knew I needed to be strong to survive this negative atmosphere. I read Dale Carnegie's *How to Win Friends and Influence People* and was immediately intrigued. The book's first page listed "12 Things This Book Will Do For *You.*" Among those things was Number 1: "Get you out of a mental rut, give you new thoughts, new visions, new ambitions." And Number 4: "Help you to win people to your way of thinking." I especially was drawn to Number 9: "Help you to handle complaints, avoid arguments, keep your human contacts smooth and pleasant." I was so convinced of the effectiveness of these methods that I enrolled in the Carnegie course by the same name.

These strategies made sense. They were logical and respectful and had helped thousands of people become more adept at managing their lives and relationships. I determined I would incorporate the strategies, too, and my first place to practice would be at my school. Specifically, I would utilize the strategies during every interaction I had with my principal, the very man who did not want me working with him. Without manipulation, but with firm resolve, I determined to earn his respect the Dale Carnegie way. After all, the principal was my professional evaluator, so, in addition to simply wanting to get along with him, I wanted him to give me a positive evaluation of my work when the time came. In the words of Malcolm X, I intended to succeed "by any means necessary." Not only did I practice Dale Carnegie's strategies on the principal, but I proactively elicited an informal evaluation from him every month. Then I followed up with a written summary of each meeting and included how I planned to incorporate his suggestions for improvement. During three years of these monthly meetings, I never received a negative evaluation from him. On the contrary, I believe he eventually came to respect my work.

My persistence paid off. After working diligently on my personal growth during the ten years I held that administrative position, I became a woman well practiced in personal strength and confidence. When I left the school, I really felt I could do absolutely anything I put my mind to, and that was a great feeling. Now, when people ask me how

I survived that intense time, I say, "With a strong spiritual foundation and by putting God in the driver's seat, a person can do anything."

*****

I Can See Clearly Now

Of course, going to litigation to settle a prejudicial matter was not a fight I was looking for, nor was it easily won, professionally or personally. But I am unequivocally glad I stood up and fought for what was right. How different my life would have been if I had turned tail and just accepted the injustice! If I had chosen the path of staying silent, would I have been ashamed of myself later? Would I have lost my self-esteem again? How might that one decision not to pursue an obvious failure of implementing a national law affect my future career, my relationships, and my parenting? I often wonder what my life would have looked like under those circumstances.

But this I do know: I had a problem to face, a serious problem that would result in lasting consequences no matter which route I took. And I faced that problem. Head on, I faced it. In the end, my seasoned persistence and my well-developed problem-solving skills combined well with God's strength to get me through another difficult time in my life.

Reflection Questions

Have you ever pursued a dream that took years of persistence, only not to achieve what you longed for?

_____

_____

_____

_____

How did you rise from the ashes of defeat?

_____

_____

_____

_____

Have you ever been the victim of discrimination in any way?

_____

_____

_____

_____

What did you do to change your situation from victim to champion?

_____

_____

_____

_____

If you did not succeed in your battle against discrimination, what mental things can you tell yourself now and what actions can you take to prevent such a future situation or make it turn out more positively?

_____

_____

_____

_____

Chapter 8

Commencement

"Many people die with their music still in them.
Why is this so? Too often it is because they are
always getting ready to live. Before they know it,
time runs out."

— Oliver Wendell Holmes

I STOOD OUTSIDE THE ivy-covered brick building that would be her home-away-from-home for four years. She stood beside me as we looked across the quad, already filled with other students also moving into their dorms. I heard her sigh. My whole world was in that sigh.

We had just unpacked the last of her suitcases into the tiny closet on her side of the small room. I had handed her the sweat pants, the tee-shirts, and the converses, and she had put them where she could grab them at a moment's notice. I was now in her world, instead of her being in mine.

The flight to Atlanta had been long—somewhat of a drawn-out exhale between her life as a child at home and her new life here as a young adult. The farewell parties had faded, the smudged packing list had been crumpled and tossed, and the tears of friends going their separate ways had flowed freely. I had stepped back, of course, refraining from my goodbye; I still had her to myself for a few days, privileged to accompany this youngest child of mine to her new academic world. I treasured the honor of helping her get settled in her dorm and of walking the campus with her. I wanted to know in my mind's eye that the Student Union was to the east of her dorm, that her English 101 class was on the top floor of the highest brick building, and that the large theater where she would spend many Friday nights listening to guest speakers or watching theatrical performances faced the west boulevard. Our final destination was the football field on the hill. Silently, we walked to the stadium, climbing the metal benches to sit for a moment, taking it all in. I could already hear her yelling, "Go, Tigers!" as she high-fived her classmates after the touchdown.

I remembered my own college days and mentally imposed them on this beloved girl, hoping she would have as many wonderful memories tucked under her arm when she walked across the amphitheater platform to receive her diploma after her years of study. I knew she would have experiences that would be uniquely her own, and I was both excited for her and a little uneasy. I remembered when freshman jitters overwhelmed me and I received my first ever "C." I remembered the girlfriend who had betrayed me after I had confided my latest crush, and the lack of sleep due to a certain 4 a.m. party. The child-now-grown would face her own challenging situations, true, but I was confident I had raised her to run after her dreams, to work hard, and to keep her priorities straight. And to call her mommy every Sunday night.

We circled back to her dorm, and now we faced the setting sun, squinting, the late afternoon breeze allowing us a moment to collect our thoughts. Intuitively, we both knew the childhood chapter of her book was closing, and we each turned toward the other at the same time. No words were needed.

We embraced, and I gave her one last peck on the cheek, turning away. Sweetly, after I had walked a few yards, she called my name and, when I glanced back, she blew me a kiss. Automatically, I "caught" the kiss in mid-air and placed it over my heart, a gesture we had shared from the time she was three years old. I turned once again, smiling through my tears.

As I walked to the rental car that would take me to the hotel, I indulged myself in memories of her childhood. Her four-year-old giggle when her two older sisters found her right away when they played hide-and-seek. Her middle school crying when her father came and went in the space of twenty minutes. Her determined gritting of her teeth when she was fifteen after I told her she must clean the bathroom again because she had done the job sloppily. My tears fell when I remembered the December evening of her senior year when she had put her arms around me as I wrote out checks to pay the bills, knowing that Christmas gifts would be simple and few. She had whispered, "It's gonna be all right, Mommy."

I opened the car door, tossed my purse on the passenger seat, and buckled up. I had been so disappointed when I'd missed a softball game due to work. I remembered the rushed mornings of braiding hair before school, the science-project poster board we finagled into the backseat of the car for the science fair, and how proud I was when she threw her graduation cap high into the air after she had received her high school diploma.

I pulled out of the university parking lot. My thoughts shifted. No one was with me in the car now. No one would fly home with me. Setting my lips into a firm line, I knew. The time had come, and I might as well get on with facing it.

As of this moment, I was officially an empty-nester.

I had always thought that that term was somewhat inaccurate and archaic, really. I was flying by myself quite well, thank you, before any of my little birds had made their appearance, and I assumed, quite naively, that I would simply slip back into my pre-nesting days of flying wherever I wanted to go, unhindered by the girls' school schedules, latest social engagements, and beloved late-night talks, which were exhausting but heartfelt nonetheless.

I boarded the plane, feigned sleep through most of the flight, and climbed into my own car, which had been left at the airport two days earlier. I still felt an odd blank sensation in the pit of my stomach. It didn't abate on the two-hour drive home as I had expected. *Pull into the driveway, turn off the engine, gather everything, and leave it all behind when you unlock that front door, Cynthia.* I inhaled deeply. At the click of the lock, I pushed open the front door and stepped inside.

Inside to what? I looked around the house, quiet and strangely foreign. No more music blaring at midnight from behind a closed bedroom door. No more running through the kitchen, grabbing an orange and a handful of nuts, as she raced to class after oversleeping. The beloved daughter had just begun a new chapter in her life. She was off on a new adventure.

Well, then.

I stood there in the entry and took it all in. Then I set down my suitcase, looked squarely at the reflection in the mirror above the side table, and spoke aloud. "Cynthia, time for a new chapter in your life, too. What's your new shindig going to be?"

I mulled over that question far longer than I expected, quite surprised when the feelings of sadness extended past the first week. Although I still lived with my partner, the loss of my grown child's company produced in me a loneliness I hadn't anticipated. When her two older sisters each had stepped into college life, I still had the youngest with me, her laughter and sarcastic remarks reminding me I was still a mother and I better not forget it. Now she, too, had entered that academic college whirlwind, and I was completely caught off-guard by my feelings. She was just… gone, and I had to mentally and emotionally adjust to the quiet, unfamiliar atmosphere in our home.

A month went by. Then two. I was having trouble shaking the loneliness, and a new restlessness appeared. A few weeks passed before I could put a name to it.

I was unfulfilled.

I had always referred to myself not as a "working mother," but as a "mother, working." Mothering had always come first, and I realized now that it had defined much more of my identity than I knew. The children had always needed me in some way or other and, even in their young adulthood, I relished the times when our paths crossed between jobs, studies, and pizza parties. Now, without the overlay of caring for the girls, even emotionally, I felt it difficult to get my bearings.

And so I started singing the blues. Really. For a good six months, I felt my feelings ebb and flow, like the ocean's tide, and I sang every blues song I could think of to match my mood. Some days were better than others, of course, but always I had an underlying question that kept rising to the surface, urging me to catch my breath and address it.

Who was I now?

Was I just "Cynthia, working" now that I wasn't primarily mothering? No, I didn't like the sound of that. When I retired from working full-time as an assistant principal at a local high school, who would I be then? Just Cynthia? Uh, uh. Nope. That wasn't happening. I was determined never to be "Just Cynthia." I had worked too hard all my life to be "just" anything.

Slowly, my mental wheels started turning. I would be wise to consider what I would do with my newly-acquired spare time. What I had poured into my children and my students, I really wanted to pour into others. After all, *I* hadn't changed; only my circumstances had flipped. I still wanted—needed—to utilize my skills and abilities in a meaningful way.

I am highly creative, and I thrive on meaningful projects that help move people to higher goals in life. Being a high school administrator was definitely challenging, but the position had given me little opportunity for any creative outlet for my unique gifts, values, and personality. Now, with my own children living independently, I began to feel somewhat stifled, held down, and increasingly disenchanted with my role in formal education. With all that I put into my days, my work had still become a daily job instead of a meaningful career, and I became increasingly disenchanted.

My restlessness extended into the nights, questions about the future bubbling up in my mind as soon as I lay my head down on my pillow. In the morning, when I became fully conscious, the questions rolled back like a dull drumbeat. *"What now? What now? What now?"*

One evening, after checking my alarm for the next day, I climbed into bed, and pushed the question away as sleep drifted in. Soon I began to dream, but this dream was different than any other dream. It was vivid, bright, and markedly dimensional. I saw myself teaching students, but not in a traditional classroom setting. Nor was I teaching the typical studies associated with high school students. Then I noticed something else: I was fully engaged, teaching with an earnestness that spoke of something more lasting, more enduring, to pass on to future generations.

I awoke. The vision lingered, not fading as ordinary dreams do. I had the odd sensation that the scene was interrupted, that the ending depended on an answer I was to give.

I went downstairs to prepare my morning tea. The dream showed me I was still a teacher, but I could also sense I was being asked to use my experiences as an educator in a different, more unique way. I felt I was being invited to participate in something. Back in the day, when I was a child attending church with my grandmother, this sensation was a "call." I smiled at the memory of hands clapping to a gospel beat, and people shouting "Amen!" as the pastor preached. Well, if this was a "call," what was I being called *to*? I filled the teakettle, put it on the burner, and turned on the heat.

I knew that our students today experienced a growing academic and digital divide between minority and white students. The cause wasn't accurately pinpointed, but the evidence was stark and unquestionable. Without a doubt, many young black students could benefit greatly from more specialized instruction. The teakettle whistled; I turned off the heat, silencing the high note. I reached for my favorite teacup and saucer on the counter, an Earl Grey teabag from the canister, and the small pitcher of cream from the fridge. I poured the boiling water directly into the cup, foregoing the teapot and dipping the Earl Grey teabag once, twice, three times before tossing it into the trashcan by the table.

We already had schools, yet we were still failing our black students. As an administrator, I knew the district had no available funds to develop extra programs. *Well, then.* I poured the cream into the tea and stirred—smiling at the small pleasure of seeing the dark brown brew turn a light creamy tan—and set the spoon on the saucer. *What to do?* I sipped the hot drink and waited for more thoughts to come.

And come they did. I set down my empty teacup. The question was answered. *I guess I'll just have to create a new program myself!*

I went to work that day, and the next and the next. But now, every time I had a moment to myself, I jotted down a thought here, a question there, and scribbled possible topics to research. At night, I lay down with ideas simmering in my head, and awoke more lighthearted than I had in months. Ah, the restlessness was draining away—I could feel it. I smiled more at the secretary and greeted the principal cheerfully.

A program developed beneath my pen as I continued to gather information. I would provide enrichment courses in reading, writing, and technology to elementary school students, and we would meet on Saturday mornings. Each student would pay $50 for eight weeks of academics, long enough to supplement the students' regular studies, but not so long as to overwhelm the students for an entire semester. Soon the program was complete, at least on paper. I named it Saturday Academy, and I was thrilled.

However, ideas must turn into reality, and reality requires working capital. Tuition would cover only basic supplies;

classroom rent and teacher salaries must still be provided. I presented the program to leaders at one of our local churches. To my surprise, they enthusiastically welcomed the idea and immediately provided classroom space. As an extra bonus, they recruited students from their own Sunday school to attend the academy.

We were off and running.

To keep the financial overhead down, I volunteered my own time—forfeiting any salary—to getting the program off the ground. Marketing was tough, and I discovered that recruiting students and hiring teachers required more time than I could afford while I was still working full-time at the high school. Within two months, dark circles had formed under my eyes from lack of sleep, and my "to-do" list was as long as my arm. It was time to make a change. I decided, with only slight hesitation, that I would officially retire from the school district in June to devote myself to the academy fulltime. Once that decision was made, I gladly shifted my energy to tying up loose ends at the school and preparing to broaden my work at the academy.

As assistant principal at the high school, I had the opportunity to supervise the senior graduating class each year. In 2003, the year I retired, I decided I would walk down the aisle myself alongside my last graduating class. That walk was symbolic for me: Somehow, I, too, had graduated. A chapter in my life was over, and a new chapter was beginning. As I climbed the three steps to the platform to take my place behind the lectern and officially open the ceremony that afternoon, I felt unmistakably that it was one of those moments when the clouds part and total clarity arises. I knew without a doubt that the "call" those many years ago meant that my life was intended for something more. I'm sure I had influenced others while I was at the school, and I was absolutely convinced I had influenced my own children. But now I knew with certainty that those years and skills were meant to combine to create something destined to make a great impact on the lives of others beyond my immediate circle. I also knew the *next* chapter in my life, whatever it was, was bound to be exciting. No longer did I dread that empty time of wandering and searching. This time I would trust that a new adventure would unfold.

And it did. It wasn't long before, in addition to running Saturday Academy, I began to rub shoulders with other retirees, and I found we had much more in common than only a cessation of working for decades. These new friends also had sparks of skills and desires that had nearly been put out by too much time on their hands, dwelling on their aches and pains and problems with grown children.

Well, I knew what to do about that. I started stirring up those burning coals of skills and desires until I saw a fire in the eyes of those gray-headed friends. I reminded them how much knowledge and wisdom they still had to offer in today's world. I encouraged them to follow the passions that had been there all along, and I let them know that, unquestionably, now was the time to make a difference in society. I could feel my own passion for life flowing through me as I looked into their eyes, seeing the same questions I had only recently asked myself.

One day, I was sipping some Earl Grey at a local coffee shop while reading an article in the *American Association of University Women* titled "Why So Few? Women in Science, Technology, Engineering, and Mathematics." A light bulb went off in my head. In an instant, I decided to join the growing movement to help close the gender gap in the sciences. My experience had shown me that not only did a gap exist between races, but also between male and female students. And especially in the sciences.

Now everything came together: All my previous training as a teacher, counselor, and administrator had prepared me for this new endeavor. With renewed enthusiasm and direction, I vigorously focused my energies, skills, and experiences on again developing Saturday courses in science, but restructuring the non-profit Saturday Academy toward a new purpose. I called the new program Amazing Girls Science, this time focusing on recruiting only girls, igniting in them from an early age—kindergarten through twelfth grade—a spark for science, technology, engineering, art, and math, otherwise known as STEAM. That first year in the science conference, we enrolled fifty girls, ranging in age from ten to thirteen.

The program grew wildly. Today, we impact the lives of over five hundred girls *each year* with our science conferences, robotic programs, computer science courses, and cryptography classes. We include courses called "Girls Who Code," and we sponsor "Hackathons"—events in which students engage in collaborative computer programming. We even developed our own local Makerspace. Parents began to tell me their daughters exhibited greater confidence in life, having developed greater self-esteem, and that they heard new excitement around the dinner table in family conversations.

Because of my work developing the academy, my name was submitted to CBS television for its program *Fulfilling the Dream*. In short order, CBS sent a crew out to the school to interview me and videotape the students. The story proved to be great promotion for the program, letting a wider audience know how focusing girls on specific subjects when they're young can help close the gender gap in the workplace when they're older, positively impacting even more lives. I was thrilled with the exposure. Word spread quickly, and in 2013, I was honored to receive the Woman of Innovations Award from the Connecticut Technology Council.

Most recently, I was nominated for the AARP (American Association of Retired Persons) Purpose Prize. The worldwide organization requested letters from people familiar with my work with the girls, and I was excited to have the opportunity to spread the word about the school. I asked those who knew about my work to write about their observations of the program. Grateful for their help, I submitted those letters and several transcripts. Within a few weeks, I was notified that I was one of five people selected out of 700 nominations. I received the award at an elaborate gala event in Chicago. Wanting to know more, AARP sent a video crew to our town for an entire day to interview and videotape me and the students in our Amazing Girls Science program.

The night of the gala, I looked around at the crowd and I knew—I just *knew*—I had made a difference in the world. I was thrilled to be around people who publicly and proudly acknowledged that the years after retiring can be some of our most productive and meaningful times. I so wholeheartedly agreed.

When the evening's program began, I listened attentively to the emcee, and then heard her call my name to come to the platform. To thunderous applause, I rose from my chair and happily made my way to the front of the ballroom and onto the stage where I was honored to receive the inaugural AARP Purpose Prize, presented by Soledad O'Brien. As I looked out over the crowd, still clapping to honor me and my work, I was overjoyed.

*****

I Can See Clearly Now

I count the entire journey after my retirement as an awesome experience, one that undoubtedly provided the fulfillment for which I had been looking. Although I worked hard to get Amazing Girls Science up and running—and it has been *a lot* of work—seeing young girls excel at something they thought was beyond their reach has been my real paycheck. Although I'm grateful and humbled by the public awards, those plaques on my wall only symbolize the true reward I have experienced: the fulfillment that comes from giving wholeheartedly to others.

Reflection Questions

Have you ever been at a crossroads in your life when you didn't know what to do with yourself or how to bring yourself out of a slump?

_____

_____

_____

_____

What did you do to change things?

_____

_____

_____

_____

What sorts of outstanding needs do you see in your community?

_____

_____

_____

_____

What could you do to help make a difference?

_____

_____

_____

_____

Are you retired or planning to retire soon? What sorts of plans will you make so you can make the best out of your retirement, even turning it into a season of refirement?

_____

_____

_____

_____

Chapter 9

From Fantasy to Fact

*"If you want to be happy, set a goal that
commands your thoughts, liberates your energy,
and inspires your hopes."*

— Andrew Carnegie

I LOVE TO TRAVEL—ALWAYS have. Working at the same
job five days a week, often taking work home from
the classroom, challenged me, and seeing the same
walls, the same desks, and the same students was fulfilling
to me. I not only influenced lives day by day, but I also
discovered that my own skills and sense of identity were
often reinforced, and I grew to enjoy the daily routine of
it all.

But, oh, I lived for the vacations. I figured that if I
worked hard, I deserved to play hard—and I worked *very*
hard. Every summer, I made sure I had reservations to go
someplace I had never been before; it seemed my hunger

for new sites and new cultures could never be fully satisfied. Vacations never exhausted me; instead, I would return to the classroom rejuvenated and refreshed, eager to share with my students my adventures and experiences.

But always, in the back of my mind, there hummed a faint murmur of lands farther away. I never spoke of it because I was having so much fun exploring the United States, but I often whispered to myself, "Someday, I will travel the world."

I didn't dwell on the dream; it didn't seem like the right time in my life to invest any time, energy, or effort into planning. I didn't know how or when or by what means that dream might come true, but that faint murmur always remained.

Those were the days when most people took the train to visit loved ones or caught a flight for business purposes to destinations within America. And, of course, the airlines had a corner on the market for international travel. But then cruise ships began to rise in popularity, and the ocean began to take on an inviting ambience. Occasionally at work, a faculty member would return from vacation, telling tales of cruising on the Caribbean for ten days. I was intrigued.

I have always loved the water, and seasickness has never affected me. Instead, the short boat rides I had taken to Long Island only whetted my appetite for more travel on the ocean. On the water, the everyday pictures of life in the classroom and life in a household melted seamlessly into just plain life, the moments blending imperceptibly into the ocean swells. Today, whenever I see the dark-blue deep that goes on as far as the eye can see, I remember it was created before any man breathed on the earth, and I am inexpressibly awed by the history of it all. Yet, at the same time, I am humbly honored to be part of that same creation. I love the sea.

Soon the murmur of the dream took on a tune, but it was still faint, and I didn't explore it further. But I did let my mind rest in those thoughts from time to time. Some would call traveling the world a fantasy—something out of reach, unreal, even silly. And my fantasy was explicit: I wanted to visit exotic ports of call around the world on luxurious cruise ships. I love to be pampered, and when my colleagues told me about the bountiful food, the welcome room service, and the attentive staff, my weary body, which had just stayed up way too late grading papers, ached for that kind of attention.

But I spoke to no one; I considered such a dream too far out of reach, and I purposely would hum another tune when the cruise ship melody rose up in me. I didn't want to get my hopes up, and I knew better than to dwell on something that seemed impossible to obtain. So the volume on the tune went down and the dream lay dormant for many years.

Then I retired.

I found myself oddly adrift—such an apt term for my ocean-loving spirit. Being around students for decades had been a busy life, and I had loved every minute of it. But when it halted, so did my identity as an administrator. No one greeted me at 7:30 a.m. with, "Good morning, Dr. Barnett." No one called to schedule appointments, to ask my opinion on new programs, or to settle disputes between teachers and parents. My skills were utilized only minimally at home and, although I knew it was time to address this new chapter of my life, I was having some trouble shifting gears. Certainly, I didn't want to become one of those people who stopped working only to die within months of the retirement party! Life was too full of possibilities for me to allow that to happen. Most of my dilemma was simply examining myself again—like when I was a teenager—to see who I really was inside and what I really wanted to do. Happily, I began to hear that murmur of the dream turn into a tune again. And the volume was going up.

One day, my companion told me that a few people from his work were making plans to take a cruise. Would I be interested? *Would I be interested?* I didn't hesitate at all. Of course, I was interested! We began making plans that evening.

And the cruise was every bit as wonderful as I had dreamed! A vacation like this was convenient in every way. Once we were onboard, we enjoyed unlimited delicious food, wonderful entertainment, upscale accommodations, and daily opportunities to visit new places. Not only did I rest physically on vacation, but I rested mentally, knowing that all these arrangements had been made by someone else, and I could simply relax and enjoy everything. I was definitely sold on cruising, and I was eager to go again.

However, cruising can be expensive, and I really, really wanted to see the world, so I knew that just this one cruise couldn't possibly quench my thirst for traveling. Every time a documentary came on TV about a foreign land, I would stop what I was doing and pay close attention. What if I could experience those lands for real? In person? Perhaps more than once? Could I really visit the Bahamas, tour cities on the Mediterranean coast, and witness for myself Alaska's majestic mountains? Could I? *Could I?*

I thought back to other times when I had thought something was impossible, out of reach, a fantasy. And then I remembered that—every time—I had found a way to make the dream come true. Every. Single. Time.

Now the melody was growing louder, like a crescendo in a wonderful piece by Strauss. It was a lovely tune, and I recognized the three-quarter timing of a waltz. Surely, I could dance to this tune; after all, I love to waltz! Finally, I let myself listen to the music, and the song now took on lyrics.

What if cruise vacations could be obtained for free?

I thought about that for a while. If I could somehow obtain cruise passage for free, the biggest obstacle to my dream would be solved. I really concentrated now. Is it possible? *Well,* I told myself, *I won't know unless I find out.*

I pursued the question with great fervor. Interestingly, I found several books on the subject and carefully read every one. Indeed, opportunities did exist to fill positions on cruise ships in exchange for free passage! My thinking was working overtime. Still, I wasn't sure how to break into this kind of gig. It wasn't quite the same as interviewing for a job or auditioning for a place in an orchestra.

I decided I would expand my research into personal investigation: I would celebrate my retirement by booking a cruise. That was the first step, to be a paying customer to enjoy the cruise *and* to find out more. Second step: Contact the cruise company to request a time slot to make a presentation on helping its guests reach their full potential.

And then I waited. Life seems to be full of opportunities to wait.

One day I checked my email to find a response to my inquiry. The company had suggested I contact the cruise director once I boarded. Nothing could be done in advance and without the cruise director's permission on the specific voyage.

Wonderful, I thought. *I can enjoy the cruise yet still have a plan.* With a light heart, I entered the days of the cruise on my calendar, arranged for my flight to the departure site, and began to pack. I could hardly wait to soak up the sun on the deck after a late breakfast in my room and walk the promenade in the late afternoon.

The day of the cruise, I stepped onto the deck of the *Dawn*, almost giddy with anticipation. Here I was, about to "sail the ocean blue," and I could feel my excitement rising with every passenger who boarded, with every salute from the crew, and with the final blast of the horn. *Bon voyage!*

But I remembered my purpose and, as soon as I was settled in my stateroom—I had a lovely starboard cabin— and we were out of the harbor, I approached the cruise director. I introduced myself and told him of my previous correspondence with the cruise line.

I had my plan well thought out in advance, and I was prepared. My strategic goal was to obtain evaluations of my presentations so I could break into the cruise lecturing circuit. But I utilized the strategies in the Dale Carnegie course I had taken many years earlier and explained to the director that I would love to help his guests further enjoy their cruising experience by presenting a brief talk, "How to Live Your Best Life," my message about reaching one's potential. Such a universal topic would apply to everyone on board, of course, and I assured him I would tailor the presentation to his specifications.

It worked. We were cruising during the hurricane season, so when one of the scheduled lecturers failed to show up one day due to the bad weather, I was asked to take her place and offer a lecture on goal-setting. I was happy to comply. I was completely familiar with that topic, and could speak with confidence, so I stepped in easily, presenting for three successive days. The talks were a hit, and I was surrounded by guests who came up to me after each session to ask questions. I was thrilled! My plan was working, and I was again in my element—teaching others and helping them gain new information in an area of great value.

Soon afterward, I received a "hire" recommendation from the cruise director, setting me up for future assignments. *Bon voyage*, again! And again!

I have been a cruise lecturer for many years now. My companion and I travel all over the world at the expense of the cruise lines. All the amenities included in the fare of regular passengers are free to my companion and me. This wonderful exchange of my time, skills, and experience for free passage to exotic ports around the world, enjoying the lifestyle of the rich and famous, is truly my dream come true.

I have found that lecturing on a cruise ship is like the chorus of a song that repeats after each verse: I educate people while I explore the world. Then I develop lecture content from my explorations so I may educate people. My background of over thirty years in education is a great asset. That experience, paired with knowing how to research topics, locations, and history, makes for great confidence in speaking to my audience of passengers.

My official title is "Destination Lecturer," and I give a series of original presentations that illustrate the culture, history, and geography of the regions, countries, and ports of call on a given cruise itinerary. I include information on anthropology, wildlife, marine life, and politics. I provide guests with insights not available in the average tourist guidebook. And I am careful to interject some humor here and there. I love to see their smiles.

It's not a bad gig, for sure. I get to travel the world, sometimes sailing to exotic places I otherwise would have never been able to visit. And what a bonus to learn about the destinations! It fits right into my love of learning and teaching, and meeting new people is a lovely experience.

Of course, I get to enjoy all those amenities that come with the cruise. An attentive steward makes up my cabin twice a day. I eat my fill of satisfying or—even better—gourmet fare around the clock, delivered directly to my stateroom if I wish. And I never cook or wash a dish! I might work three hours a week and have people applaud me at the end of every presentation.

My assignments have indeed taken me around the world, visiting such destinations as the Mediterranean, the Caribbean, Alaska, and Hawaii. I meet and spend time with business executives, physicians, athletes, entertainers, writers, journalists, scientists, and government officials. I attend concerts, read good books, soak in the Jacuzzi, exercise in the health club, cool off in the swimming pool, and nearly every evening enjoy a large Broadway-type show. Of course, I also drink in the simple pleasure of settling into a chair, watching the ocean, and occasionally glimpsing some marine creatures frolicking in the ship's wake. I gaze at the sky and breathe deeply the salty air. When we are in a port of call, the time is mine to explore the land if I like, or to relax on board if I prefer.

Shipboard life is great fun, and the demands on my time aren't particularly heavy. I think of it as a win-win-win situation. My win is obvious—my dream has come true—and the cruise line wins by offering a low-cost service to its customers. The passengers win by learning something new about their destinations.

The song is a familiar melody now, and I sing it often, moving slowly to the waltz of the sea.

*****

I Can See Clearly Now

This dream was with me for quite some time, always in the back of my mind, keeping me company for many years. But I didn't actively work on bringing it to fruition until I felt the timing was right. When that time came, I clarified my dream and put it into words. Then I drew on my creative skills and researched the matter from every angle. I had a dream and I worked hard to make it come true. And it did. Somehow, working hard to make a dream come true seems to make the realization of that dream even sweeter.

Sometimes, dreams change along the way, and that's okay. Sometimes, dreams must be put on hold for a while, and that's okay too. What is *not* okay is giving up on dreams. That is never okay.

My advice to all dreamers? Work hard and never, ever give up on your dream.

Reflection Questions

Have you ever traveled? What did you learn from these experiences? Most importantly, what did you learn about yourself?

_____

_____

_____

_____

What big dream do you have right now that you keep putting on the back burner?

_____

_____

_____

_____

Make a list of five things you can do right now to move toward making that dream a reality.

1. _____
2. _____
3. _____
4. _____
5. _____

A Final Note

The Story Continues...

*"Only put off for tomorrow what you are willing
to die left undone."*

— Pablo Picasso

AS YOU CAN see by the title of this book, I'm not
done yet! Even though I am seventy-six years old,
I'm not done yet! Even though I have raised three
daughters and enjoyed two full careers, I'm not done yet!
And even though I have traveled the world and won national
awards, I'm not done yet!

And you don't need to be done yet either!

I still have dreams and plans, and I plan to *still* use my
creative problem-solving skills to overcome future obstacles.
I figure obstacles will come no matter how old I get, so I'd
better be prepared now.

And you'd better be too!

These smaller stories, of course, are only a small part of the bigger story of my life. My hope is that they prompt you to think about what strengthens you in *your* life. I am now independent and self-assured, but as you know, that wasn't always the case. Here are a few of the things I learned that I really, really want you to know:

- I rarely did it all alone; I often had help.

- I never gave up.

- Sometimes, my obstacles were of my own making; sometimes, others put obstacles in my way. Either way, I discovered that creativity, persistence, and aid—when needed—are the keys to overcoming all of life's challenges.

- If we overcome life's obstacles and squarely face life's challenges, we are free to live our dreams.

Be inspired! Be refired!

Cynthia Barnett

About the Author

D<small>R. C</small>YNTHIA BARNETT is a nationally recognized author, speaker, and coach. Her "refirement message" has been featured in *US News and World Report*, local newspapers, and TV shows. She was recently featured in *The Wall Street Journal* and in *TIME* magazine in its lead article about women in mid-life who have reinvented themselves. She is the recipient of the inaugural AARP Purpose Prize, which recognizes people over the age of fifty who have "used their wisdom and experience to revitalize their lives and make the world a better place." She is a leading authority on how to "refire and reinvent, making dreams come true."

Cynthia is currently living a refired life, paying it forward through her nonprofit program for girls, Amazing Girls Science, to help them ignite a spark for STEAM (science, technology, engineering, art, and math). She resides in Connecticut.

www.refiredontretire.com

Book Dr. Cynthia to Speak at Your Next Event

WHEN IT COMES to choosing a professional speaker for your next event, you will find no one more respected or successful—no one who will leave your audience or colleagues with a more renewed passion for life—than Dr. Cynthia.

Whether your audience is 10 or 10,000, Dr. Cynthia can deliver a customized message of inspiration for your meeting or conference. Dr. Cynthia understands your audience does not want to be "taught" anything, but is rather interested in hearing stories of inspiration, achievement, and real-life people stepping into their destinies.

As a result, Dr. Cynthia's speaking philosophy is to entertain and inspire your audience with passion and stories proven to help people achieve extraordinary results. If you are looking for a memorable speaker who will leave your audience wanting more, contact Dr. Cynthia today!

www.refiredontretire.com

drcynthia@refiredontretire.com

203-807-3321

Claim Your Complimentary 30-Minute Life Vision Strategy Session

I F YOU ARE feeling stuck in your life and finding it hard to get out of your own way regarding your health, career, finances, relationships, or all of the above, allow Dr. Cynthia to coach you to live a happier, more balanced, and more abundant life.

To schedule your free Life Vision Strategy Session and learn more about Dr. Cynthia's coaching services, visit:

www.RefireDontRetire.com

Quotes to Inspire, Empower, and Challenge You to Be Your Best

"Our deepest fear is not that we are inadequate. Our deepest fear is that we are powerful beyond measure. It is our light, not our darkness that most frightens us."

— Marianne Williamson

"Ninety-nine percent of all failures come from people who have a habit of making excuses."

— George Washington Carver

"Life is like a combination lock: your job is to find the right numbers in the right order so you can have anything you want."

— Brian Tracy

"Many people die with their music still in them."

— Oliver Wendell Holmes

"If we did all the things we are capable of doing, we would literally astound ourselves."

— Thomas Edison

"The greatest danger for most of us is not that our aim is too high and we miss it, but that it is too low and we reach it."

— Michelangelo

"Alone we can do so little; together we can do so much."

— Helen Keller

"There is a difference between interest and commitment. When you're interested in doing something, you do it only when it's convenient. When you are committed to something, you accept no excuses, only results."

— Ken Blanchard

"None of us can change our yesterdays, but all of us can change our tomorrows."

— Colin Powell

"Your heart is born free, have the courage to follow it"

— William Wallace

"Tell everyone what you want to do and someone will want to help you"

— W. Clement Stone

"It takes as much energy to wish as it does to plan"

— Eleanor Roosevelt

"Be thankful for what you have; you'll end up having more. If you concentrate on what you don't have, you will never, ever have enough."

— Oprah Winfrey

"You may not control all the events that happen to you, but you can decide not to be reduced by them."

— Maya Angelou

"Never be limited by other people's limited imaginations."

— Dr. Mae Jemison

"Change does not roll in on the wheels of inevitability, but comes through continuous struggle."

— Martin Luther King Jr.